Cookies & Pies

D1372495

PUBLICATIONS INTERNATIONAL, LTD.

Manufactured in U.S.A.

8   7   6   5   4   3   2   1

ISBN: 0-517-06677-7

This edition published by
Crescent Books
Distributed by Outlet Book Company, Inc.
A Random House Company
225 Park Avenue South
New York, New York 10003

This edition published by Publications International, Ltd., 7373 North Cicero Avenue, Lincolnwood, Illinois 60646.

Pictured on the front cover *(from left to right):* Chocolate Peanut Butter Cup Cookies *(page 48);* Lola's Apple Pie *(page 56).*

Pictured on the back cover *(clockwise from top left):* Oatmeal Shaggies *(page 36);* Cherry City Amaretto Cherry Cream Pie *(page 83);* Butter-Flavored Brickle Drizzles *(page 11).*

Microwave ovens vary in wattage and power output; cooking times given with microwave directions in this book may need to be adjusted.

Cookies & Pies

To discover the best cookie recipes in America, Butter Flavor Crisco holds a cookie-baking contest at a major state or county fair in each of the 50 states.

This national cookie-baking contest is truly unique because the majority of contestants are parent-child partners. What fun as moms, dads, grandparents, children and grandchildren team up in kitchens across the country to create exciting new cookie recipes! Each state picks a cookie category — chocolate chip, peanut butter or oatmeal — and the state winners are then judged by a national panel of baking experts who chose the grand prize winner — *The American Cookie!*

★★★★

The American Pie Celebration began in 1986 to commemorate Crisco's 75th anniversary of serving good food to families everywhere. Its popularity has grown at both the state and national levels, and the celebration has now become an annual event to pay tribute to the great American tradition of pie baking.

To search out the best pie recipes across America, a Crisco pie baking contest is held at a major state or county fair in each of the 50 states. Bakers compete in a pie category usually chosen by each fair to reflect the unique personality of that state, including its native grown ingredients. The winner from each contest is entered into a national competition for the first place "Silver Rolling Pin" award and title of "Baker of The American Pie." To date, over 7,000 pie bakers have submitted their best pies hoping to win the grand prize of a brand new kitchen!

We hope that these delicious cookie and pie recipes will tempt you to enter the Crisco American Baking Celebration competition in your state. To find out the location and date of your state competition, write to:

The Crisco Kitchens
P.O. Box 5547
Cincinnati, Ohio 45201

Cookies

Top: Choco-Scutterbotch (page 20);
Right: Chewy Oatmeal-Apricot-Date Bars
(page 34)

TIPS FOR COOKIE SUCCESS FROM THE CRISCO KITCHEN

★ ★ ★ ★

General guidelines

• Read the entire recipe before beginning to make sure you have all the necessary ingredients and baking utensils.

• Measure all the ingredients accurately and assemble them in the order called for in the recipe.

• Prepare pans and baking sheets according to the recipe directions. Adjust the oven racks and heat the oven before starting to bake. Check the oven temperature for accuracy with a mercury oven thermometer.

• Follow the recipe directions and baking times exactly. Check for doneness using the test given in the recipe.

• Add 1 tablespoon milk or water for each ½ cup Butter Flavor Crisco when converting a recipe calling for butter or margarine.

Measuring

• Use standardized graduated measuring cups for measuring all dry ingredients and ingredients like Butter Flavor Crisco, peanut butter, sour cream, yogurt, nuts, dried fruit, marshmallow creme, coconut, chopped fresh fruit, preserves and jams. Fill the correct measuring cup to overflowing and level it off with the straight edge of metal spatula or knife.

• Use standardized glass or plastic liquid measuring cups with a pouring spout to measure all liquid ingredients. Place the cup on a flat surface, fill to the desired mark and check the measurement at eye level.

• Use standardized graduated measuring spoons, not eating or serving spoons, for measuring small amounts of ingredients. For dry ingredients, fill the correct measuring spoon to overflowing and level it off with the straight edge of a metal spatula or knife.

- Lightly spoon flour into the correct measuring cup and then level it off with the straight edge of a metal spatula or knife. Do not tap or bang the measuring cup or dip the measuring cup into the bag as this will pack the flour. Too much flour can make cookies dry.

- Press brown sugar into the correct measuring cup and level it off with the straight edge of a metal spatula or knife. It should hold the shape of the cup when turned out. Use light brown sugar unless otherwise stated.

- Press Butter Flavor Crisco into the correct measuring cup. Cut through with a metal spatula or knife and press again to eliminate air pockets. Level with the straight edge of a metal spatula or knife.

- Use large eggs unless stated otherwise.

Baking

- Use shiny, sturdy aluminum baking sheets with little or no sides. They allow the heat to circulate easily during baking and promote even browning. Cookies baked on insulated baking sheets may need 1 to 2 minutes longer baking time.

- Bake only one baking sheet at a time in the center of the oven. If the cookies brown unevenly, rotate the baking sheet from front to back halfway through the baking time. If you do use more than one sheet at a time, rotate the baking sheets from top to bottom halfway through the baking time. Space oven racks 6 inches apart. Allow baking sheets to cool between batches; the dough will spread if placed on a hot baking sheet.

- Watch cookies carefully to avoid overbaking. Check them at the minimum baking time, then check them often to make sure they don't overbake. Follow the recipe for yield and size since the baking time is determined for that size cookie.

- Remove cookies from the baking sheets immediately after baking and place in a single layer on wire racks to cool, unless otherwise specified. Always cool cookies completely before stacking and storing. Bar cookies may be cooled and stored in the baking pan.

Storage

- Store cooled cookies at room temperature in airtight containers unless otherwise specified in the recipe. Store each kind separately to prevent changes in flavor and texture. Freeze baked cookies in airtight containers or freezer bags for up to six months.

Cookie Classics

★ CHILD'S CHOICE ★

Debbie and Garret Smith, Cascade, Montana
*Garret (age 8) and his mom, Debbie, filled these cookies with every
kind of goodie they could think of.*

2⅓ cups all-purpose flour
  1 cup Butter Flavor Crisco®
  1 teaspoon baking soda
  ½ teaspoon baking powder
  1 cup granulated sugar
  1 cup firmly packed brown sugar
  2 eggs
  1 teaspoon maple flavor

  2 cups Quaker® Oats (quick or
    old fashioned), uncooked
  ¾ cup Hershey®s Semi-Sweet
    Chocolate Chips
  ¾ cup Reese's® Peanut Butter
    Chips
  ¾ cup miniature marshmallows

1. Heat oven to 350°F. Grease baking sheet with Butter Flavor Crisco.

2. Combine flour, Butter Flavor Crisco, baking soda and baking powder in
large bowl. Beat at low speed of electric mixer until blended. Increase speed to
medium. Mix thoroughly. Beat in granulated sugar, brown sugar, eggs and
maple flavor. Add oats. Stir in chocolate chips, peanut butter chips and
marshmallows with spoon until well blended.

3. Shape dough into 1½-inch balls. Flatten slightly. Place 2 inches apart on
greased baking sheet.

4. Bake at 350°F for 9 to 10 minutes or until light golden brown. Cool 1
minute on baking sheet before removing to cooling rack.

Makes 3½ dozen cookies

★ BUTTER-FLAVORED ★ BRICKLE DRIZZLES

Judy and John Repplinger, Sheridan, Oregon
Judy and her son John, 15, decided their cookies won the blue ribbon at the Oregon State Fair because they are moist and chewy, yet at the same time crunchy.

COOKIES

1 cup Butter Flavor Crisco®
1 cup granulated sugar
1 cup firmly packed brown sugar
1 can (14 ounces) sweetened condensed milk (not evaporated milk)
1 teaspoon vanilla

1¾ cups all-purpose flour
1 teaspoon salt
½ teaspoon baking soda
3 cups Quick Quaker® Oats, uncooked
1 cup almond brickle chips

DRIZZLE

1 cup Hershey's Milk Chocolate Chips

1. Heat oven to 350°F. Grease baking sheet with Butter Flavor Crisco.

2. **For cookies,** combine Butter Flavor Crisco, granulated sugar and brown sugar in large bowl. Stir with spoon until well blended and creamy. Stir in condensed milk and vanilla. Mix well.

3. Combine flour, salt and baking soda. Stir into creamed mixture. Stir in oats.

4. Shape dough into 1-inch balls. Press tops into brickle chips. Place brickle side up 2 inches apart on greased baking sheet.

5. Bake at 350°F for 9 to 10 minutes or until set but not browned. Remove to cooling rack. Cool completely.

6. **For drizzle,** place chocolate chips in heavy resealable sandwich bag. Seal. Microwave at 50% (MEDIUM). Knead bag after 1 minute. Repeat until smooth (or melt by placing in bowl of hot water). Cut tiny tip off corner of bag. Squeeze out and drizzle over cookies. *Makes 6 dozen cookies*

★ OATMEAL COOKIES ★

Joan and Karlie Pagano, Tulsa, Oklahoma
*Joan and seven-year-old Karlie really had a third member of the
family on their team at the Tulsa State Fair; Joan's mother
provided inspiration, support and guidance during the creation of
this prize-winning cookie.*

1¼ cups Butter Flavor Crisco®
¾ cup firmly packed brown sugar
3 tablespoons milk
1 teaspoon water
½ teaspoon vanilla
½ teaspoon coconut flavor
1 egg

1¼ cups all-purpose flour
1 teaspoon baking soda
¾ teaspoon salt
3 cups Quaker® Oats (quick or
    old fashioned), uncooked
½ cup pecan pieces
½ cup raisins

1. Heat oven to 325°F.

2. Combine Butter Flavor Crisco, brown sugar, milk, water, vanilla and coconut flavor in large bowl. Beat at medium speed of electric mixer until well blended. Beat in egg.

3. Combine flour, baking soda and salt. Add gradually to creamed mixture at low speed. Mix until well blended. Stir in oats, nuts and raisins with spoon. Drop by rounded teaspoonfuls 2 inches apart onto ungreased baking sheet.

4. Bake at 325°F for 10 to 12 minutes or until slightly browned and slightly moist in center. Cool 2 minutes on baking sheet before removing to cooling rack.
Makes 5 dozen cookies

SNICKERDOODLES

2 cups sugar, divided
1 cup Butter Flavor Crisco®
2 eggs
2 tablespoons milk
1 teaspoon vanilla

2¾ cups all-purpose flour
2 teaspoons cream of tartar
1 teaspoon baking soda
¾ teaspoon salt
2 teaspoons cinnamon

1. Heat oven to 400°F.

2. Combine 1½ cups sugar, Butter Flavor Crisco, eggs, milk and vanilla in large bowl. Beat at medium speed of electric mixer until well blended.

3. Combine flour, cream of tartar, baking soda and salt. Add gradually to creamed mixture at low speed. Mix just until blended. Shape dough into 1-inch balls.

4. Combine remaining ½ cup sugar and cinnamon in small bowl. Roll balls of dough in mixture. Place 2 inches apart on ungreased baking sheet.

5. Bake at 400°F for 7 to 8 minutes. Remove to cooling rack.

Makes 6 dozen cookies

Hint: Cinnamon-sugar mixture can be put in resealable plastic bag. Put 2 to 3 dough balls at a time in bag. Seal. Shake to sugar-coat dough.

VARIATION

Colored Sugar Snickerdoodles: Add the 2 teaspoons cinnamon to flour mixture in Step 3. Combine 3 tablespoons colored sugar and 3 tablespoons granulated sugar. Use for coating instead of cinnamon-sugar mixture.

★ PEANUT BUTTER CHOCOLATE ★ CHIP COOKIES

Teri and Nicholas Redding, Sibley, Louisiana
It was 12-year-old Nicholas who convinced his mother, Teri, to join him in a mother/son baking team, which produced this prize-winning cookie.

1 cup plus 1 tablespoon Butter
    Flavor Crisco®, divided
1 cup slivered almonds
¾ cup granulated sugar
¾ cup firmly packed brown sugar
¾ cup Jif® Creamy Peanut Butter
1 teaspoon vanilla
½ teaspoon almond extract

1 teaspoon water
2 eggs
2¼ cups all-purpose flour
1 teaspoon baking powder
1 teaspoon salt
1 package (12 ounces) Hershey's
    Semi-Sweet Chocolate Chips
    (2 cups)

1. Heat oven to 350°F.

2. Place 1 tablespoon Butter Flavor Crisco and nuts in baking pan. Place in 350°F oven to melt shortening. Stir well. Stir every 2 minutes until nuts are light golden brown. Remove from oven. Cool completely.

3. Combine remaining 1 cup Butter Flavor Crisco, granulated sugar, brown sugar, peanut butter, vanilla, almond extract and water in large bowl. Beat at medium speed of electric mixer until well blended. Add eggs. Beat until blended.

4. Combine flour, baking powder and salt. Add gradually to creamed mixture at low speed. Mix just until blended. Stir in nuts and chocolate chips with spoon. Drop by rounded tablespoonfuls 2 inches apart onto ungreased baking sheet.

5. Bake at 350°F for 10 to 12 minutes or until light golden brown. Remove to cooling rack.

Makes 3½ to 4 dozen cookies

★ BRIAN'S BUFFALO COOKIES ★

Vickie and Brian Vaughan, Sparks, Nevada
Brian's Buffalo Cookies were named the Chocolate Chip National Winner at the 1991 Butter Flavor Crisco American Cookie Celebration.

1 cup Butter Flavor Crisco®, melted
1 cup granulated sugar
1 cup firmly packed brown sugar
2 tablespoons milk
1 teaspoon vanilla
2 eggs
2 cups all-purpose flour
1 teaspoon baking powder
1 teaspoon baking soda
½ teaspoon salt
1 cup Quaker® Oats (quick or old fashioned), uncooked
1 cup corn flakes, crushed to about ½ cup
1 cup Hershey's Semi-Sweet Chocolate Chips
½ cup chopped pecans
½ cup flake coconut

1. Heat oven to 350°F. Grease baking sheet with Butter Flavor Crisco.

2. Combine Butter Flavor Crisco, granulated sugar, brown sugar, milk and vanilla in large bowl. Beat at low speed of electric mixer until well blended. Add eggs. Beat at medium speed until well blended.

3. Combine flour, baking powder, baking soda and salt. Add gradually to creamed mixture at low speed. Stir in oats, corn flakes, chocolate chips, nuts and coconut with spoon. Fill ice cream scoop that holds ¼ cup with dough (or use ¼ cup measure). Level with knife. Drop 3 inches apart onto greased baking sheet.

4. Bake at 350°F for 13 to 15 minutes or until lightly browned around edges but still slightly soft in center. Cool 3 minutes on baking sheet before removing to cooling rack with wide, thin pancake turner.   *Makes 2 to 2½ dozen cookies*

★ RAISIN-APPLE OATMEAL COOKIES ★

Mary and Katelin Lair, Bloomington, Minnesota
*Mary and Katelin were totally surprised at having their cookies
named best oatmeal cookies at the Minnesota State Fair.*

1 cup Butter Flavor Crisco®
1 cup granulated sugar
1 cup firmly packed brown sugar
2 eggs
1 teaspoon vanilla
2⅓ cups all-purpose flour
1 teaspoon baking powder
1 teaspoon baking soda
½ teaspoon nutmeg

¼ teaspoon ground cloves
2 cups Quick Quaker® Oats,
  uncooked
1 large Granny Smith apple,
  peeled and chopped (about
  1⅓ cups)
½ cup raisins
½ cup chopped walnuts

1. Heat oven to 375°F. Grease baking sheet with Butter Flavor Crisco.

2. Combine Butter Flavor Crisco, granulated sugar and brown sugar in large bowl. Beat at medium speed of electric mixer until well blended. Beat in eggs and vanilla.

3. Combine flour, baking powder, baking soda, nutmeg and cloves. Add gradually to creamed mixture at low speed. Stir in oats, apple, raisins and nuts with spoon. Shape dough into 1½-inch balls. Place 2 inches apart on greased baking sheet.

4. Bake at 375°F for 13 to 14 minutes or until lightly browned. Cookies will look moist. *Do not overbake.* Cool 1 minute on baking sheet before removing to cooling rack.
Makes 3 dozen cookies

★ BREAKFAST COOKIES ★

Colleen and Anne Liebhart, Kirksville, Missouri
*Colleen and her 10-year-old daughter, Anne, have always worked
together in the kitchen, but this was their first entry in a
baking competition.*

1 cup Butter Flavor Crisco®
1 cup Jif® Extra Crunchy Peanut
  Butter
¾ cup granulated sugar
¾ cup firmly packed brown sugar
2 eggs, beaten
1½ cups all-purpose flour
1 teaspoon baking powder
1 teaspoon baking soda

1 teaspoon cinnamon
1¾ cups Quick Quaker® Oats,
  uncooked
1¼ cups raisins
1 medium Granny Smith apple,
  finely grated, including juice
⅓ cup finely grated carrot
¼ cup flake coconut (optional)

1. Heat oven to 350°F.

2. Combine Butter Flavor Crisco, peanut butter, granulated sugar and brown sugar in large bowl. Beat at medium speed of electric mixer until blended. Beat in eggs.

3. Combine flour, baking powder, baking soda and cinnamon. Add gradually to creamed mixture at low speed. Beat until blended. Stir in oats, raisins, apple, carrot and coconut with spoon. Drop by measuring tablespoonfuls onto ungreased baking sheet.

4. Bake at 350°F for 9 to 11 minutes or until just brown around edges. Cool 1 minute on baking sheet before removing to cooling rack.

Makes 5 to 6 dozen cookies

Hint: Freeze cookies between sheets of waxed paper in sealed container. Use as needed for breakfast on-the-run or as a nutritious snack.

★ MOM AND KATIE'S CRUNCHY ★ CHOCOLATE CHIP COOKIES

Madeleine and Katie LaJeunesse, Cincinnati, Ohio
Madeleine's family was quite surprised to hear about her and Katie's prize-winning effort. "I'm not really known for my cooking skills," she says, but in this case they brought her a blue ribbon.

1 cup Butter Flavor Crisco®	½ teaspoon salt
¾ cup firmly packed dark brown sugar	½ teaspoon nutmeg
½ cup granulated sugar	1½ cups Hershey®s Semi-Sweet Chocolate Chips
1 egg, lightly beaten	1 cup Quaker® Oats (quick or old fashioned), uncooked
1 teaspoon vanilla	1 cup finely chopped pecans
1½ cups all-purpose flour	½ cup honey crunch wheat germ
1 teaspoon baking soda	

1. Heat oven to 375°F.

2. Combine Butter Flavor Crisco, brown sugar and granulated sugar in large bowl. Beat with spoon until well blended. Mix in egg and vanilla.

3. Combine flour, baking soda, salt and nutmeg. Add to creamed mixture. Stir until well blended.

4. Combine chocolate chips, oats, nuts and wheat germ. Stir into dough. Mix well. Shape dough into 2-inch balls. Place 3 inches apart on ungreased baking sheet. Flatten with hand to about ⅜-inch thickness.

5. Bake at 375°F for 7 to 8 minutes or until golden brown. Remove to flat surface to cool.

Makes 2 to 2½ dozen cookies

★ DREAMY CHOCOLATE CHIP ★ COOKIES

Alieen Reed and Alissia Harmon, Pine Bluff, Arkansas
Alieen and Alissia may be newcomers to Pine Bluff, but the mother-daughter team obviously knows its way around a kitchen.

1¼ cups firmly packed brown
    sugar
 ¾ cup Butter Flavor Crisco®
 3 eggs, lightly beaten
 2 teaspoons vanilla
 1 package (4 ounces) German's
    sweet chocolate, melted,
    cooled
 3 cups all-purpose flour
 1 teaspoon baking soda

½ teaspoon salt
1 package (11½ ounces)
    Hershey's Milk Chocolate
    Chips
1 package (10 ounces) Hershey's
    Premium Semi-Sweet
    Chocolate Chunks
1 cup coarsely chopped
    macadamia nuts

1. Heat oven to 375°F.

2. Combine brown sugar, Butter Flavor Crisco, eggs and vanilla in large bowl. Beat at low speed of electric mixer until blended. Increase speed to high. Beat 2 minutes. Add melted chocolate. Mix until well blended.

3. Combine flour, baking soda and salt. Add gradually to creamed mixture at low speed.

4. Stir in chocolate chips, chocolate chunks and nuts with spoon. Drop by rounded tablespoonfuls 3 inches apart onto ungreased baking sheet.

5. Bake at 375°F for 9 to 11 minutes or until set. Cool 2 minutes on baking sheet before removing to cooling rack. *Makes 3 dozen cookies*

★ CHOCO-SCUTTERBOTCH ★

**Mary Fran and Rachelle Nelson,
Plymouth, New Hampshire**
*Mary Fran and her daughter, Rachelle, just recently moved from a
city of 60,000 to the small farm community of Plymouth.*

2/3 cup Butter Flavor Crisco®
1/2 cup firmly packed brown sugar
2 eggs
1 package (18.25 ounces)
Duncan Hines® Moist Deluxe
Yellow Cake Mix
1 cup toasted rice cereal

1/2 cup milk chocolate chunks
1/2 cup Hershey's Butterscotch
Chips
1/2 cup Hershey's Semi-Sweet
Chocolate Chips
1/2 cup coarsely chopped walnuts
or pecans

1. Heat oven to 375°F.

2. Combine Butter Flavor Crisco and brown sugar in large bowl. Beat at medium speed of electric mixer until well blended. Beat in eggs.

3. Add cake mix gradually at low speed. Mix until well blended. Stir in cereal, chocolate chunks, butterscotch chips, chocolate chips and nuts with spoon. Stir until well blended. Shape dough into 1¼-inch balls. Place 2 inches apart on ungreased baking sheet. Flatten slightly. Shape sides to form circle, if necessary.

4. Bake at 375°F for 7 to 9 minutes or until lightly browned around edges.
Cool 2 minutes before removing to paper towels.   *Makes 3 dozen cookies*

★ OATMEAL HONEY COOKIES ★

Sherry and Ashlie Willis, Memphis, Tennessee
*Sherry and Ashlie had one advantage in the Mid-South Fair in
Memphis— they had based their recipe on an old family recipe for
"grandma's cookies."*

1 cup Butter Flavor Crisco®
1 cup firmly packed dark brown
sugar
1 egg
1/2 cup honey
1/4 cup granulated sugar
1/4 cup water
1½ teaspoons vanilla

1½ cups all-purpose flour
1 teaspoon cinnamon
1/2 teaspoon baking soda
1/2 teaspoon salt
3 cups Quaker® Oats (quick or
old fashioned), uncooked
1 cup raisins
1/2 cup coarsely chopped pecans
continued

1. Heat oven to 350°F. Grease baking sheet with Butter Flavor Crisco.

2. Combine Butter Flavor Crisco, brown sugar, egg, honey, granulated sugar, water and vanilla in large bowl. Beat at low speed of electric mixer until blended. Increase speed to medium. Beat until light and creamy.

3. Combine flour, cinnamon, baking soda and salt. Add gradually to creamed mixture at low speed. Increase speed to medium. Beat until well blended. Stir in oats with spoon. Mix until well blended. Stir in raisins and nuts. Drop by heaping tablespoonfuls onto greased baking sheet.

4. Bake at 350°F for 11 to 12 minutes or until golden brown. Cool 3 to 5 minutes on baking sheet before removing to flat surface.

Makes 3 dozen cookies

Note: For small cookies, drop dough by heaping teaspoonfuls onto greased baking sheet. Bake at 350°F for 9 to 11 minutes. Makes 4 to 5 dozen small cookies.

★ OATMEAL TOFFEE LIZZIES ★

Jan and Elizabeth Whitaker, Crofton, Kentucky
Although Jan considers herself an accomplished chef, she had never entered a cooking competition before.

1 cup Butter Flavor Crisco®
1 cup granulated sugar
1 cup firmly packed brown sugar
2 eggs, beaten
1 tablespoon milk
1 teaspoon vanilla
2 cups all-purpose flour
1 teaspoon baking soda
1 teaspoon salt
2 cups Quick Quaker® Oats, uncooked
1 package (12 ounces) Hershey's Semi-Sweet Chocolate Chips (2 cups)
3/4 cup almond brickle chips
1/2 cup finely chopped pecans

1. Heat oven to 350°F. Grease baking sheet with Butter Flavor Crisco.

2. Combine Butter Flavor Crisco, granulated sugar and brown sugar in large bowl. Beat with spoon until well blended. Add eggs, milk and vanilla. Mix well.

3. Combine flour, baking soda and salt. Add to creamed mixture. Mix well. Stir in oats, chocolate chips, brickle chips and nuts until well blended. Shape dough into 1¼- to 1½-inch balls with lightly floured hands. Place 2 inches apart on greased baking sheet. Flatten slightly.

4. Bake at 350°F for 12 to 15 minutes or until cookies begin to brown around edges. Remove to flat surface to cool.

Makes 4½ dozen cookies

★ PEANUT BUTTER AND JELLY ★ THUMBPRINT COOKIES

Terry and Mandy Moore, Oaklyn, New Jersey
This mother-daughter team has been entering baking contests together for four years.

COOKIES

½ cup Butter Flavor Crisco®
½ cup Jif® Creamy Peanut Butter
½ cup granulated sugar
½ cup firmly packed brown sugar
1½ teaspoons vanilla
1 egg
¼ cup toasted wheat germ
¾ cup all-purpose flour

½ cup whole wheat flour
¾ teaspoon baking soda
½ teaspoon baking powder
½ teaspoon salt
1 egg white, lightly beaten
1 cup chopped cocktail peanuts
¼ cup strawberry spreadable fruit*

DRIZZLE

3 tablespoons Hershey®s Semi-Sweet Chocolate Chips

1. **For cookies,** combine Butter Flavor Crisco, peanut butter, granulated sugar, brown sugar and vanilla in large bowl. Beat with spoon until well blended. Beat in egg and wheat germ.

2. Combine all-purpose flour, whole wheat flour, baking soda, baking powder and salt. Stir into creamed mixture. Cover. Refrigerate 3 hours or overnight.

3. Heat oven to 375°F. Grease baking sheet with Butter Flavor Crisco.

4. Shape dough into ¾-inch balls. Roll in egg white and then nuts. Place 2 inches apart on greased baking sheet. Press thumb in center of each ball.

5. Bake at 375°F for 8 to 10 minutes or until set and just beginning to brown. Remove to cooling rack. Spoon ¼ teaspoon spreadable fruit into center of each hot cookie. Cool completely.

6. **For drizzle,** place chocolate chips in heavy resealable sandwich bag. Seal. Microwave at 50% (MEDIUM). Knead bag after 1 minute. Repeat until smooth (or melt by placing in bowl of hot water). Cut tiny tip off corner of bag. Squeeze out and drizzle over cookies.   *Makes 5½ to 6 dozen cookies*

*Substitute strawberry jam for spreadable fruit, if desired.

Delicious Bar Cookies

★ EMILY'S DREAM BARS ★

Michael and Emily Cacia, Indianapolis, Indiana
Emily credits teamwork between her and father, Michael, for the success of these cookies. Both teammates credit the chocolate-covered peanuts for the extra-special flavor.

1 cup Jif® Extra Crunchy Peanut Butter
½ cup Butter Flavor Crisco®
½ cup firmly packed brown sugar
½ cup light corn syrup
1 egg
1 teaspoon vanilla
1 cup all-purpose flour
½ teaspoon baking powder
¼ cup milk

2 cups 100% natural oats, honey and raisins cereal
1 package (12 ounces) Hershey's Mini Chips Semi-Sweet Chocolate (2 cups), divided
1 cup almond brickle chips
1 cup milk chocolate covered peanuts
1 package (2 ounces) nut topping (⅓ cup)

1. Heat oven to 350°F. Grease 13×9×2-inch pan with Butter Flavor Crisco.

2. Combine peanut butter, Butter Flavor Crisco, brown sugar and corn syrup in large bowl. Beat at medium speed of electric mixer until creamy. Add egg and vanilla. Beat well.

3. Combine flour and baking powder. Add alternately with milk to creamed mixture at medium speed. Stir in cereal, 1 cup chocolate chips, almond brickle chips and chocolate covered nuts with spoon. Spread in greased pan.

4. Bake at 350°F for 20 to 26 minutes or until golden brown and toothpick inserted in center comes out clean. Sprinkle remaining 1 cup chocolate chips over top immediately after removing from oven. Let stand about 3 minutes or until chips become shiny and soft. Spread over top. Sprinkle with nut topping. Cool completely. Cut into bars about 2×1 inch. *Makes 4½ dozen bars*

★ FOUR-LAYER OATMEAL BARS ★

Linda Borrego and Jaymee Borrego-Sowell, Santa Fe, New Mexico
Linda and nine-year-old Jaymee say this recipe was inspired by an apricot bar recipe made by Linda's grandmother.

OAT LAYER
- ½ cup Butter Flavor Crisco®
- 1 egg
- 1½ cups Quick Quaker® Oats, uncooked
- 1 cup firmly packed brown sugar
- ¾ cup plus 2 tablespoons all-purpose flour
- 1 teaspoon cinnamon
- ¾ teaspoon baking soda
- ¼ teaspoon salt

FRUIT LAYER
- 1½ cups sliced, peeled fresh peaches* (cut slices in half crosswise)
- ¾ cup crushed pineapple, undrained
- ¾ cup sliced, peeled Granny Smith apple (cut slices in half crosswise)
- ½ cup chopped walnuts or pecans
- ¼ cup granulated sugar
- 2 tablespoons cornstarch
- ½ teaspoon nutmeg

CREAM CHEESE LAYER
- 1 package (8 ounces) cream cheese, softened
- 1 egg
- ¼ cup granulated sugar
- ½ teaspoon fresh lemon juice
- ½ teaspoon vanilla

1. Heat oven to 350°F. Grease 11×7×2-inch glass baking dish with Butter Flavor Crisco.

2. **For oat layer,** combine Butter Flavor Crisco and egg in large bowl. Stir with fork until blended. Add oats, brown sugar, flour, cinnamon, baking soda and salt. Stir until well blended and crumbs form. Press 1¾ cups crumbs lightly into bottom of greased dish. Reserve remaining crumbs.

3. Bake at 350°F for 10 minutes. Cool completely.

4. **For fruit layer,** combine peaches, pineapple, apple, nuts, granulated sugar, cornstarch and nutmeg in medium saucepan. Cook and stir on medium heat until mixture comes to a boil and thickens. Cool completely.

5. *Increase oven temperature to 375°F.*

continued

*Diced canned peaches, well drained, can be used in place of fresh peaches.

6. **For cream cheese layer,** combine cream cheese, egg, granulated sugar, lemon juice and vanilla in medium bowl. Beat at medium speed of electric mixer until well blended. Spread over cooled oat layer. Spoon cooled fruit mixture over cheese layer. Spread gently to cover cream cheese. Sprinkle reserved crumbs over fruit.

7. Bake at 375°F for 30 minutes. Cool to room temperature. Refrigerate. Cut into bars about 2 × 1¾ inches. *Makes 20 bars*

★ OATMEAL CARAMEL DELIGHT BARS ★

Sharon and Lea Jorgenson, Waubay, South Dakota
Sharon and her 12-year-old daughter, Lea, were first-time competitors at the South Dakota State Fair this year.

1 cup granulated sugar	2 eggs
1 cup firmly packed brown sugar	3 cups Quick Quaker® Oats,
½ cup Butter Flavor Crisco®	uncooked
½ cup butter or margarine, softened	2½ cups all-purpose flour
1 teaspoon baking soda	1 package (12 ounces) Hershey's Semi-Sweet Chocolate Chips (2 cups), divided
1 teaspoon cinnamon	40 caramels, unwrapped
1 teaspoon vanilla	3 tablespoons water, divided
½ teaspoon baking powder	
½ teaspoon salt	

1. Heat oven to 375°F.

2. Combine granulated sugar, brown sugar, Butter Flavor Crisco, butter, baking soda, cinnamon, vanilla, baking powder, salt and eggs in large bowl. Beat at medium speed of electric mixer until well blended. Add oats and flour gradually at low speed. Press half (about 2½ cups) into ungreased 13 × 9 × 2-inch pan. Sprinkle with 1 cup chocolate chips.

3. Combine caramels and 1 tablespoon water in medium microwave-safe bowl. Microwave at 50% (MEDIUM) for 4 minutes or until caramels have melted (or melt on rangetop in small saucepan on very low heat). Stir occasionally. Drizzle half of mixture (about ½ cup) over chips. Crumble remaining oatmeal mixture over top. Press flat.

4. Bake at 375°F for 15 to 18 minutes, or until lightly browned.

5. Add 1 tablespoon water to remaining caramel mixture. Stir well. Reheat in microwave at 50% for 1 minute (or in saucepan). Add remaining 1 cup chocolate chips. Stir until chocolate is melted and mixture is well blended. Reheat if necessary. Stir in remaining 1 tablespoon water. Spread over hot baked surface. Cool. Cut into bars about 2¼ × 1 inch. *Makes 4 dozen bars*

★ NICOLE'S BANANA BARS ★

Debra and Nicole Chevrette, Harrisville, Rhode Island
*A morning chat about their breakfast oatmeal and bananas
ultimately produced the blue ribbon for Debra and her 8-year-old
daughter, Nicole.*

BASE

2 cups firmly packed light brown sugar
1 cup Butter Flavor Crisco®
2 eggs
1 teaspoon vanilla

2½ cups all-purpose flour
1 teaspoon baking soda
½ teaspoon salt
3 cups Quaker® Oats (quick or old fashioned), uncooked

FILLING

1 can (14 ounces) sweetened condensed milk (not evaporated milk)
2 ripe bananas, sliced
2 tablespoons Butter Flavor Crisco

1 teaspoon granulated sugar
1 teaspoon vanilla
½ teaspoon salt

1. Heat oven to 350°F. Grease 13×9×2-inch pan with Butter Flavor Crisco.

2. **For base,** combine brown sugar, 1 cup Butter Flavor Crisco, eggs and vanilla in large bowl. Beat at medium speed of electric mixer until well blended. Stir in flour, baking soda and salt with spoon. Stir in oats. Reserve one third of mixture. Press remaining into bottom of baking dish.

3. **For filling,** combine condensed milk, bananas and 2 tablespoons Butter Flavor Crisco in medium saucepan. Cook and stir constantly on low heat until mixture thickens and resembles banana pudding. Remove from heat. Stir in sugar, vanilla and salt. Spread over base. Crumble reserved oat mixture over top of filling.

4. Bake at 350°F for 25 to 30 minutes or until golden brown. Cool. Refrigerate. Cut into bars about 2¼×2 inches.   *Makes 2 dozen bars*

Note: Bars may also be served warm.

★ CHIPPY CHEESEYS ★

Virginia and Peter Spina, Jamesville, New York
*Both Virginia and her 12-year-old son, Peter, claim they invented
the name of this winner, chewy chocolate chip cookies with a creamy
cheesecake layer.*

BASE

1¼ cups firmly packed brown
   sugar
¾ cup Butter Flavor Crisco®
1 egg
2 tablespoons milk
1 tablespoon vanilla

2 cups all-purpose flour
1 teaspoon salt
¾ teaspoon baking soda
1 cup Hershey's Mini Chips
   Semi-Sweet Chocolate
1 cup finely chopped walnuts

FILLING

2 packages (8 ounces each) cream
   cheese, softened
2 eggs

¾ cup granulated sugar
1 teaspoon vanilla

1. Heat oven to 375°F. Grease 13×9×2-inch pan with Butter Flavor Crisco.

2. **For base,** combine brown sugar and Butter Flavor Crisco in large bowl. Beat at medium speed of electric mixer until creamy. Beat in 1 egg, milk and 1 tablespoon vanilla.

3. Combine flour, salt and baking soda. Add gradually to creamed mixture at low speed. Stir in chocolate chips and nuts with spoon. Spread half of dough in greased pan.

4. Bake at 375°F for 8 minutes.

5. **For filling,** combine cream cheese, 2 eggs, granulated sugar and 1 teaspoon vanilla in medium bowl. Beat at medium speed of electric mixer until smooth. Pour over hot crust.

6. Roll remaining dough into 13×9-inch rectangle between sheets of waxed paper. Remove top sheet. Flip dough over onto filling. Remove waxed paper.

7. Bake at 375°F for 40 minutes or until top is set and light golden brown. Cool to room temperature. Cut into bars about 2×1¾ inches. Refrigerate.
Makes 2½ dozen bars

Chippy Cheeseys

★ PEANUT BUTTER BARS ★

Lois and Ryan Mahoney, Casper, Wyoming
Ryan, 8, claims his mother is the family chocoholic, but Lois insists that it was Ryan's idea to use chocolate in their prize-winning entry.

BASE

²/₃ cup Jif® Creamy Peanut Butter
½ cup Butter Flavor Crisco®
¾ cup firmly packed brown sugar
½ cup granulated sugar
2 eggs
1 teaspoon vanilla

1½ cups all-purpose flour
½ teaspoon baking soda
¼ teaspoon salt
1 cup Quick Quaker® Oats,
  uncooked

PEANUT BUTTER LAYER

1½ cups confectioners sugar
2 tablespoons Jif® Creamy
  Peanut Butter

1 tablespoon butter or
  margarine, softened
3 tablespoons milk

CHOCOLATE GLAZE

2 squares (1 ounce each)
  Hershey's Unsweetened
  Baking Chocolate

2 tablespoons butter or
  margarine

1. Heat oven to 350°F. Grease 13×9×2-inch pan with Butter Flavor Crisco.

2. **For base,** combine ²/₃ cup peanut butter and Butter Flavor Crisco in large bowl. Beat at medium speed of electric mixer until blended. Add brown sugar and granulated sugar. Beat until well blended. Add eggs and vanilla. Beat until well blended.

3. Combine flour, baking soda and salt. Stir into creamed mixture with spoon. Stir in oats. Press into bottom of greased pan.

4. Bake at 350°F for 20 minutes or until golden brown. Cool to room temperature.

5. **For peanut butter layer,** combine confectioners sugar, 2 tablespoons peanut butter, 1 tablespoon butter and milk. Mix with spoon until smooth. Spread on base. Refrigerate 30 minutes.

6. **For chocolate glaze,** combine chocolate and 2 tablespoons butter in microwave-safe measuring cup. Microwave at 50% (MEDIUM). Stir after 1 minute. Repeat until smooth (or melt on rangetop in small saucepan on very low heat). Cool slightly. Spread over peanut butter layer. Cut into bars about 3×1½ inches. Refrigerate about 1 hour or until set. Let stand 15 to 20 minutes at room temperature before serving. *Makes 2 dozen bars*

Peanut Butter Bars

★ CHEWY OATMEAL-APRICOT-DATE ★ BARS

Nina and Louise Bevilacqua, Haverhill, Massachusetts
This artistic mother-and-daughter team believes that "there is no better art form than fine food" and proved it by creating a masterpiece that won the blue ribbon.

COOKIES

1¼ cups firmly packed brown sugar
¾ cup plus 4 teaspoons Butter Flavor Crisco®
3 eggs
2 teaspoons vanilla
2 cups Quick Quaker® Oats, uncooked, divided
½ cup all-purpose flour
2 teaspoons baking powder

1 teaspoon cinnamon
¼ teaspoon nutmeg
¼ teaspoon salt
1 cup finely grated carrots
1 cup finely minced dried apricots
1 cup minced dates
1 cup finely chopped walnuts
⅔ cup Hershey's Vanilla Milk Chips

FROSTING

1 package (3 ounces) cream cheese, softened
¼ cup Butter Flavor Crisco®
2½ cups confectioners sugar
1 to 2 teaspoons milk

¾ teaspoon lemon extract
½ teaspoon vanilla
½ teaspoon finely grated lemon peel
⅓ cup finely chopped walnuts

1. Heat oven to 350°F. Grease 13×9×2-inch pan with Butter Flavor Crisco. Flour lightly.

2. **For cookies,** combine brown sugar and ¾ cup plus 4 teaspoons Butter Flavor Crisco in large bowl. Beat at medium speed of electric mixer until fluffy. Add eggs, one at a time, and vanilla. Beat until well blended and fluffy.

3. Process ½ cup oats in food processor or blender until finely ground. Combine with flour, baking powder, cinnamon, nutmeg and salt. Add gradually to creamed mixture at low speed. Add remaining 1½ cups oats, carrots, apricots, dates, 1 cup nuts and vanilla milk chips. Mix until partially blended. Finish mixing with spoon. Spread in greased pan.

4. Bake at 350°F for 35 to 45 minutes or until center is set and cookie starts to pull away from sides of pan. Toothpick inserted in center should come out clean. *Do not overbake.* Cool completely.

5. **For frosting,** combine cream cheese, ¼ cup Butter Flavor Crisco, confectioners sugar, milk, lemon extract, vanilla and lemon peel in medium bowl. Beat at low speed until blended. Increase speed to medium-high. Beat until fluffy. Spread on baked surface. Cut into bars about 2¼×2 inches. Refrigerate.

Makes 2 dozen bars

Extra Special Cookies

★ OATMEAL SHAGGIES ★

**Carolyn McPharlin and Jessica Hoffmann,
Salt Lake City, Utah**
*Ten-year-old Jessica grew the carrots for these chewy cookies in her
part of the family garden.*

COOKIES
- 2 cups Quick Quaker® Oats, uncooked
- 1 cup finely shredded carrots
- 1 cup firmly packed brown sugar
- 1 cup raisins
- 1 cup all-purpose flour
- 1 teaspoon baking powder
- 1 teaspoon baking soda
- 1 teaspoon salt
- ½ teaspoon cinnamon
- ½ teaspoon cloves
- 2 eggs, beaten
- ½ cup Butter Flavor Crisco®, melted and cooled
- ⅓ cup milk
- 1 cup shredded coconut
- ½ cup finely chopped walnuts

FROSTING
- 1 cup confectioners sugar
- 2 tablespoons butter or margarine, softened
- 2 teaspoons grated orange peel
- 1 tablespoon plus 1 teaspoon Citrus Hill® Orange Juice

1. Heat oven to 350°F. Grease baking sheet with Butter Flavor Crisco.

2. **For cookies,** combine oats, carrots, brown sugar and raisins in large bowl.

3. Combine flour, baking powder, baking soda, salt, cinnamon and cloves. Stir into oat mixture with spoon.

4. Combine eggs, Butter Flavor Crisco and milk. Stir into carrot mixture. Stir in coconut and nuts. Drop by rounded tablespoonfuls 2½ inches apart onto greased baking sheet.

5. Bake at 350°F for 10 to 12 minutes or until lightly browned. Remove to cooling rack. Cool completely.

6. **For frosting,** combine confectioners sugar, butter, orange peel and orange juice in small bowl. Stir until smooth and good spreading consistency. Frost cookies.

Makes 2½ to 3 dozen cookies

Oatmeal Shaggies

★ RASPBERRY FRECKLES ★

Diane and Susan Tite, Marine City, Michigan
Diane, who won the blue ribbon with her daughter Susan, has been entering baked goods in the Michigan State Fair since 1964.

COOKIES

1 cup sugar
½ cup Butter Flavor Crisco®
1 egg
1 tablespoon raspberry-flavored liqueur
2⅔ cups all-purpose flour
1 teaspoon baking powder
½ teaspoon baking soda

½ teaspoon salt
½ cup dairy sour cream
1 cup cubed (⅛ to ¼ inch) white confectionery coating
¾ cup Hershey®s Mini Chips Semi-Sweet Chocolate
½ cup (2¼-ounce bag) crushed, sliced almonds

TOPPING

¼ cup seedless red raspberry jam
1 teaspoon raspberry-flavored liqueur

⅓ cup chopped white confectionery coating
2 teaspoons Butter Flavor Crisco®

1. Heat oven to 375°F. Grease baking sheet with Butter Flavor Crisco.

2. **For cookies,** combine sugar and ½ cup Butter Flavor Crisco in large bowl. Stir with spoon until well blended. Stir in egg and 1 tablespoon liqueur.

3. Combine flour, baking powder, baking soda and salt. Add alternately with sour cream to creamed mixture. Stir in cubed confectionery coating, chocolate chips and nuts.

4. Roll dough to ¼-inch thickness on floured surface. Cut with 3-inch scalloped round cutter. Place 2 inches apart on greased baking sheet.

5. Bake at 375°F for 7 minutes or just until beginning to brown. Cool 2 minutes on baking sheet before removing to paper towels. Cool completely.

6. **For topping,** combine raspberry jam and 1 teaspoon liqueur in microwave-safe measuring cup or bowl. Microwave at 50% (MEDIUM) until jam melts (or melt on rangetop in small saucepan on very low heat). Drop mixture in 10 to 12 dots to resemble freckles on top of each cookie.

7. Combine chopped confectionery coating and 2 teaspoons Butter Flavor Crisco in heavy resealable sandwich bag. Seal. Microwave at 50% (MEDIUM). Knead bag after 1 minute. Repeat until smooth (or melt by placing in bowl of hot water). Cut tiny tip off corner of bag. Squeeze out and drizzle over cookies.

Makes 3 dozen cookies

★ FROSTED PEANUT BUTTER ★ PEANUT BRITTLE COOKIES

Claudia and Verne Cysensky, Tacoma, Washington
These peanutty treats were the Grand Prize Winner at the 1991 Butter Flavor Crisco American Cookie Celebration.

PEANUT BRITTLE
1½ cups granulated sugar
1½ cups shelled unroasted Spanish peanuts
¾ cup light corn syrup
½ teaspoon salt

1 tablespoon Butter Flavor Crisco®
1½ teaspoons vanilla
1½ teaspoons baking soda

COOKIES
½ cup Butter Flavor Crisco®
½ cup granulated sugar
½ cup firmly packed brown sugar
½ cup Jif® Creamy Peanut Butter
1 tablespoon milk

1 egg
1⅓ cups all-purpose flour
¾ teaspoon baking soda
½ teaspoon baking powder
¼ teaspoon salt

FROSTING
1¼ cups Reese's® Peanut Butter Chips

Reserved 1 cup crushed peanut brittle

1. **For peanut brittle,** grease 15½ × 12-inch baking sheet with Butter Flavor Crisco.

2. Combine 1½ cups granulated sugar, nuts, corn syrup and 1½ teaspoon salt in 3-quart saucepan. Cook and stir on medium-low heat until 240°F on candy thermometer.

3. Stir in 1 tablespoon Butter Flavor Crisco and vanilla. Cook and stir until 300°F on candy thermometer. Watch closely so mixture does not burn.

4. Remove from heat. Stir in 1½ teaspoons baking soda. Pour onto greased baking sheet. Spread to ¼-inch thickness. Cool. Break into pieces. Crush into medium-fine pieces to measure 1 cup. Set aside.

5. Heat oven to 375°F.

6. **For cookies,** combine ½ cup Butter Flavor Crisco, ½ cup granulated sugar, brown sugar, peanut butter and milk in large bowl. Beat at medium speed of electric mixer until well blended. Beat in egg.

7. Combine flour, ¾ teaspoon baking soda, baking powder and ¼ teaspoon salt salt. Add gradually at low speed. Mix until well blended.

continued

Frosted Peanut Butter Peanut Brittle Cookies

8. Shape dough into 1¼-inch balls. Place 3½ inches apart on ungreased baking sheet. Flatten into 3-inch circle.

9. Bake at 375°F for 8 to 9 minutes or until light brown. Cool 2 minutes on baking sheet before removing to flat surface. Cool completely.

10. **For frosting,** place peanut butter chips in microwave-safe measuring cup or bowl. Microwave at 50% (MEDIUM). Stir after 1 minute. Repeat until smooth (or melt in saucepan on very low heat). Spread frosting on half of each cookie.

11. Sprinkle reserved crushed peanut brittle over frosting. Refrigerate to set quickly or let stand at room temperature. *Makes 2 dozen cookies*

★ PEACH-STUFFED OATMEAL ★ ALMOND COOKIES

Sherry and Christina Kemp, Elk Grove, California
Sherry says she's always been drawn by the creative possibilities in baking but admits that she and her daughter, Christina, were surprised to take top honors in this, their first baking competition.

COOKIES
½ cup plus 2 tablespoons butter or margarine, softened, divided
2½ cups Quaker® Oats (quick or old fashioned), uncooked
1 cup sugar
½ cup Butter Flavor Crisco®
1 can (12½ ounces) almond filling, divided
1 egg, lightly beaten
1 tablespoon plus 1½ teaspoons Citrus Hill® Orange Juice
1 tablespoon half-and-half
1½ cups all-purpose flour

FILLING
1 large fresh peach, peeled and mashed
½ cup sugar
1 tablespoon peach schnapps
½ teaspoon fresh lemon juice
Reserved almond filling

GARNISH
1 cup Hershey's Semi-Sweet Chocolate Chips
1 package (2 ounces) blanched almonds, ground (½ cup)

1. **For cookies,** melt 2 tablespoons butter in large skillet on medium heat. Add oats. Stir until oats are lightly browned. Turn out onto paper towels. Cool completely.

2. Combine 1 cup sugar, Butter Flavor Crisco and remaining ½ cup butter in large bowl. Beat at low speed of electric mixer until fluffy.

3. Place ⅔ cup almond filling in small bowl. Stir in, one at a time, egg, orange juice and half-and-half. Stir until well blended. Add to creamed mixture at low speed.

4. Stir one fourth of flour at a time into creamed mixture with spoon. Stir in oats. Cover. Place in freezer until dough is very firm.

5. **For filling,** combine peach, ½ cup sugar, schnapps and lemon juice in small saucepan. Cook and stir on medium heat until thick and glossy. Reserve 2 tablespoons. Cool mixture in saucepan completely. Add remaining almond filling (about ½ cup) to saucepan. Stir until well blended.

6. Heat oven to 350°F. Line baking sheet with parchment paper.

7. Shape dough into 1-inch balls. Place 2 inches apart on parchment paper. Flatten slightly.

8. Bake at 350°F for 9 to 12 minutes or just until barely golden. Cool 2 minutes on baking sheet before removing to cooling rack. Cool completely.

9. Place ¼ teaspoon peach filling on each bottom of half of the cookies. Top with remaining cookies. Press together gently. Press outside edges of cookies together. Brush one side of all sandwiched cookies with reserved 2 tablespoons peach mixture.*

10. **For garnish,** place chocolate chips in microwave-safe cup or bowl. Microwave at 50% (MEDIUM). Stir after 1 minute. Repeat until smooth (or melt by placing in small saucepan on very low heat). Spread edge of cookies with chocolate and then roll lightly in nuts. Place on waxed paper, glazed side up, until chocolate is set.   *Makes 4 dozen sandwich cookies*

*Stir ¼ teaspoon water into peach mixture if too thick.

PEANUT BUTTER SENSATIONS

1 cup Jif® Creamy Peanut Butter	1 egg
¾ cup granulated sugar	1¼ cups all-purpose flour
½ cup firmly packed brown sugar	¾ teaspoon baking soda
½ cup Butter Flavor Crisco®	½ teaspoon baking powder
1 tablespoon milk	¼ teaspoon salt
1 teaspoon vanilla	

1. Heat oven to 375°F.

2. Combine peanut butter, granulated sugar, brown sugar, Butter Flavor Crisco, milk and vanilla in large bowl. Beat at medium speed of electric mixer until well blended. Beat in egg.

3. Combine flour, baking soda, baking powder and salt. Add gradually to creamed mixture at low speed. Mix just until blended. Drop by rounded tablespoonfuls 2 inches apart onto ungreased baking sheet. Make crisscross marks on top with floured fork tines.

4. Bake at 375°F for 8 to 10 minutes. Cool 2 minutes on baking sheet before removing to cooling rack.   *Makes 2 dozen cookies*

★ HEAVENLY OATMEAL HEARTS ★

Mary and Nicole Severson, Minot, North Dakota
Six-year-old Nicole loves to help her mom in the kitchen and says baking and playing golf are two of her favorite activities.

COOKIES

1 cup plus 2 tablespoons Butter Flavor Crisco®
1 cup firmly packed brown sugar
1/2 cup granulated sugar
2 eggs
1 teaspoon vanilla
1 1/2 cups plus 1/3 cup all-purpose flour
1 1/2 teaspoons baking soda
3/4 teaspoon salt

3 cups Quaker® Oats (quick or old fashioned), uncooked
1 cup Hershey's Milk Chocolate Chips
1 cup Hershey's Vanilla Milk Chips
1 cup plus 2 tablespoons cinnamon roasted peanuts,* chopped

DRIZZLE

1/2 cup Hershey's Milk Chocolate Chips
1/2 cup Hershey's Vanilla Milk Chips

1 teaspoon Butter Flavor Crisco®, divided

1. Heat oven to 375°F.

2. **For cookies,** combine 1 cup plus 2 tablespoons Butter Flavor Crisco, brown sugar and granulated sugar in large bowl. Beat at medium speed of electric mixer until light and fluffy. Beat in eggs and vanilla.

3. Combine flour, baking soda and salt. Add gradually to creamed mixture at low speed. Mix until well blended. Stir in oats, 1 cup chocolate chips, 1 cup vanilla milk chips and nuts with spoon.

4. Place 3-inch heart-shaped cookie cutter on ungreased baking sheet. Place 1/3 cup dough inside cutter. Press to edges and level. Remove cutter. Repeat to form remaining cookies. Space 2 1/2 inches apart.

5. Bake at 375°F for 9 minutes or until light golden brown. Cool on baking sheet until slightly warm before removing to cooling rack. Cool completely.

6. **For drizzle,** place 1/2 cup chocolate chips and 1/2 cup vanilla milk chips in separate heavy resealable sandwich bags. Add 1/2 teaspoon Butter Flavor Crisco to each bag. Seal. Microwave at 50% (MEDIUM). Knead bag after 1 minute. Repeat with each bag until smooth (or melt by placing each in bowl of hot water). Cut tiny tip off corner of each bag. Squeeze out and drizzle over cookies. To serve, cut in half, if desired. *Makes 22 heart cookies*

*Substitute honey roasted peanuts and 1 1/2 teaspoons cinnamon if cinnamon roasted peanuts are unavailable.

★ JEREMY'S FAMOUS TURTLES ★

Louise and Jeremy Kopasz, Pueblo, Colorado
Jeremy and his grandmother made these cookies which were named the Oatmeal National Winner at the 1991 Butter Flavor Crisco American Cookie Celebration.

COOKIES

3 egg whites
1 egg yolk
1¼ cups Butter Flavor Crisco®
¾ cup firmly packed brown sugar
½ cup granulated sugar
1 teaspoon vanilla
1¾ cups all-purpose flour
1 teaspoon baking soda
¾ teaspoon salt
½ cup Hershey's Butterscotch Chips
½ cup Hershey's Semi-Sweet Chocolate Chips

½ cup chopped dates
½ cup chopped pecans
½ cup diced dried fruit bits
⅓ cup cinnamon applesauce
¼ cup toasted wheat germ
¼ cup ground shelled sunflower seeds
2 tablespoons honey
3 cups Quaker® Oats (quick or old fashioned), uncooked
8 ounces pecan halves (2 cups)

COATING

1 to 2 egg whites, lightly beaten   ½ cup granulated sugar

1. **For cookies,** place 3 egg whites in medium bowl. Beat at medium speed of electric mixer until frothy. Beat in egg yolk until well blended.

2. Combine Butter Flavor Crisco, brown sugar and granulated sugar in large bowl. Beat at medium speed until well blended. Add egg mixture and vanilla. Beat until well blended.

3. Combine flour, baking soda and salt. Add gradually to creamed mixture at low speed. Stir in with spoon, one at a time, butterscotch chips, chocolate chips, dates, chopped nuts, fruit bits, applesauce, wheat germ, sunflower seeds, honey and oats. Cover. Refrigerate dough 1 hour.

4. Heat oven to 350°F. Grease baking sheet with Butter Flavor Crisco.

5. Shape dough into 1½-inch balls. Cut pecan halves into 4 lengthwise pieces for legs. Save broken pieces for heads and tails

6. **For coating,** dip top of cookie ball in beaten egg white, then dip in sugar. Place sugar side up 2½ inches apart on greased baking sheet. Insert lengthwise nut pieces for legs. Flatten slightly. Place nut sliver for tail and rounded nut piece for head.

7. Bake at 350°F for 9 to 11 minutes or until lightly browned. Reposition nuts, if necessary. Cool 30 seconds on baking sheet before removing to paper towels.
Makes 7½ dozen cookies

★ CHOCOLATE PEANUT BUTTER ★ CUP COOKIES

Maria and Jenna Baldwin, Mesa, Arizona
Jenna and her mother, Maria, won the blue ribbon at the Arizona State Fair over a number of other competitors, including Jenna's nine-year-old sister, Kathryn.

COOKIES

1 cup Hershey's Semi-Sweet Chocolate Chips
2 squares (1 ounce each) Hershey's Unsweetened Baking Chocolate
1 cup sugar
½ cup Butter Flavor Crisco®
2 eggs

1 teaspoon salt
1 teaspoon vanilla
1½ cups plus 2 tablespoons all-purpose flour
½ teaspoon baking soda
¾ cup finely chopped peanuts
36 miniature Reese's® Peanut Butter Cups, unwrapped

DRIZZLE

1 cup Reese's® Peanut Butter Chips

1. Heat oven to 350°F.

2. **For cookies,** combine chocolate chips and chocolate squares in microwave-safe measuring cup or bowl. Microwave at 50% (MEDIUM). Stir after 2 minutes. Repeat until smooth (or melt on rangetop in small saucepan on very low heat). Cool slightly.

3. Combine sugar and Butter Flavor Crisco in large bowl. Beat at medium speed of electric mixer until blended and crumbly. Beat in eggs, one at a time, then salt and vanilla. Reduce speed to low. Add chocolate slowly. Mix until well blended. Stir in flour and baking soda with spoon until well blended. Shape dough into 1¼-inch balls. Roll in nuts. Place 2 inches apart on ungreased baking sheet.

4. Bake at 350°F for 8 to 10 minutes or until set. Press peanut butter cup into center of each cookie immediately. Press cookie against cup. Cool 2 minutes on baking sheet before removing to cooling rack. Cool completely.

5. **For drizzle,** place peanut butter chips in heavy resealable sandwich bag. Seal. Microwave at 50% (MEDIUM). Knead bag after 1 minute. Repeat until smooth (or melt by placing bag in hot water). Cut tiny tip off corner of bag. Squeeze out and drizzle over cookies.   *Makes 3 dozen cookies*

ULTIMATE CHOCOLATE CHIP COOKIES

1¼ cups firmly packed brown
    sugar
¾ cup Butter Flavor Crisco®
2 tablespoons milk
1 tablespoon vanilla
1 egg

1¾ cups all-purpose flour
1 teaspoon salt
¾ teaspoon baking soda
1 cup Hershey's Semi-Sweet
    Chocolate Chips
1 cup coarsely chopped pecans*

1. Heat oven to 375°F.

2. Combine brown sugar, Butter Flavor Crisco, milk and vanilla in large bowl. Beat at medium speed of electric mixer until well blended. Beat in egg.

3. Combine flour, salt and baking soda. Add gradually to creamed mixture at low speed. Mix just until blended. Stir in chocolate chips and nuts with spoon. Drop by rounded tablespoonfuls 3 inches apart onto ungreased baking sheet.

4. Bake at 375°F for 8 to 10 minutes for chewy cookies (they will look light and moist — *do not overbake*), 11 to 13 minutes for crisp cookies. Cool 2 minutes on baking sheet before removing to cooling rack.   *Makes 3 dozen cookies*

*Substitute an additional ½ cup chocolate chips for the pecans, if desired.

VARIATIONS

Drizzle: Combine 1 teaspoon Butter Flavor Crisco® and 1 cup Hershey's Semi-Sweet Chocolate Chips or 1 cup coarsely chopped white confectioners coating in microwave-safe measuring cup or bowl. Microwave at 50% (MEDIUM). Stir after 1 minute. Repeat until smooth (or melt on rangetop in small saucepan on very low heat). To thin, add a little more Butter Flavor Crisco. Drizzle over cookies. Sprinkle with nuts before chocolate sets, if desired. Place cookies in refrigerator for a few minutes to set, if desired.

Chocolate-Dipped: Melt chocolate as directed for Drizzle. Dip one end of cooled cookie halfway up in chocolate. Sprinkle with finely chopped nuts before chocolate sets. Place on waxed paper until chocolate is firm. Place cookies in refrigerator for a few minutes to set, if desired.

Pies

*Top: **Arizona's Supreme Citrus Pie** (page 71);*
*Right: **Chocolate Chip Pecan Pie** (page 84)*

CLASSIC CRISCO CRUST

8-, 9- OR 10-INCH SINGLE CRUST

1⅓ cups all-purpose flour
½ teaspoon salt
½ cup Crisco® Shortening
3 tablespoons cold water

8- OR 9-INCH DOUBLE CRUST

2 cups all-purpose flour
1 teaspoon salt
¾ cup Crisco® Shortening
5 tablespoons cold water

10-INCH DOUBLE CRUST

2⅔ cups all-purpose flour
1 teaspoon salt
1 cup Crisco® Shortening
7 to 8 tablespoons cold water

1. Spoon flour into measuring cup and level. Combine flour and salt in medium bowl.

2. Cut in Crisco using pastry blender (or 2 knives) until all flour is blended to form pea-size chunks.

3. Sprinkle with water, 1 tablespoon at a time. Toss lightly with fork until dough will form a ball.

For Single Crust Pies

4. Press dough between hands to form a 5- to 6-inch "pancake." Flour rolling surface and rolling pin lightly. Roll dough into circle.

5. Trim 1 inch larger than upside-down pie plate. Loosen dough carefully.

6. Fold dough into quarters. Unfold and press into pie plate. Fold edge under. Flute.

For Baked Pie Crusts

1. For recipes using a baked pie crust, heat oven to 425°F. Prick bottom and sides thoroughly with fork (50 times) to prevent shrinkage.

2. Bake at 425°F for 10 to 15 minutes or until lightly browned.

For Unbaked Pie Crusts

1. For recipes using an unbaked pie crust, follow baking directions given in that recipe.

For Double Crust Pies

1. Divide dough in half. Roll each half separately. Transfer bottom crust to pie plate. Trim edge even with pie plate.

2. Add desired filling to unbaked pie crust. Moisten pastry edge with water. Lift top crust onto filled pie. Trim ½ inch beyond edge of pie plate. Fold top edge under bottom crust. Flute. Cut slits in top crust to allow steam to escape. Bake according to specific recipe directions.

CONTEMPORARY TECHNIQUES

Food Processor Method

1. Place Crisco, water and flour in processor bowl. Sprinkle salt over flour.

2. Process 3 to 5 seconds until dough just forms. Shape into ball.

Note: For flakier crust, freeze Crisco in tablespoon-size chunks before processing.

Waxed Paper Method

1. Flour "pancake" lightly on both sides.

2. Roll between sheets of waxed paper (or plastic wrap) on dampened countertop. Peel off top sheet.

3. Flip dough into pie plate. Remove other sheet.

DECORATIVE TIPS

Rope Edge

Fold overhang under and make stand-up edge. Press thumb into pastry at an angle. Pinch pastry between thumb and knuckle of index finger, rolling knuckle towards thumb. Place thumb in groove left by finger and repeat.

Cutouts

Trim edge even with pie plate. Cut desired shapes (about ¾ inch in size) from remaining pastry using tiny cookie cutter, thimble or bottlecap. Moisten pastry edge. Place cutouts on pastry edge, slightly overlapping. Press into place.

Woven Lattice Top

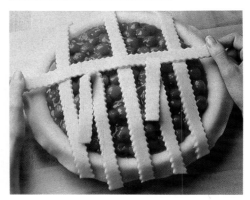

1. Leave overhang on bottom crust. Cut top crust into ten ½-inch strips. Place 5 strips evenly across filling. Fold every other strip back. Lay first strip across in opposite direction.

2. Continue in this pattern, folding back every other strip each time you add a cross strip.

3. Trim ends of lattice strips even with crust overhang. Press together. Fold edge under. Flute.

Down~Home Pies

★ LOLA'S APPLE PIE ★

Lola Mefferd, Bellflower, California
Lola has always considered baking pies her "virtuoso performance."

CRUST
10-inch Classic Crisco® Double
Crust

FILLING
8 to 9 cups thinly sliced, peeled
Granny Smith or other tart
apples (about 3 pounds or
9 medium)
¾ to 1 cup sugar
2 tablespoons all-purpose flour

1 teaspoon cinnamon
⅛ teaspoon allspice
⅛ teaspoon cloves
⅛ teaspoon salt
2 tablespoons butter or
margarine

TOPPING
Sugar

1. **For crust,** prepare (see pages 52–53). Roll and press bottom crust into 10-inch pie plate. Do not bake. Heat oven to 400°F.

2. **For filling,** place apples in large bowl. Combine ¾ to 1 cup sugar, flour, cinnamon, allspice, cloves and salt. Sprinkle over apples. Toss to coat. Spoon into unbaked pie crust. Dot with butter. Moisten pastry edge with water.

3. Roll top crust same as bottom. Lift onto filled pie. Trim ½ inch beyond edge of pie plate. Fold top edge under bottom crust. Flute. Cut slits or shapes in top crust to allow steam to escape.

4. **For topping,** sprinkle with sugar.

5. Bake at 400°F for 50 to 55 minutes or until filling in center is bubbly and crust is golden brown. Cover edge with foil, if necessary, to prevent overbrowning. Serve barely warm or at room temperature.   *One 10-inch pie*

★ DELAWARE BLUEBERRY PIE ★

Loretta Wootten, Velton, Deleware
"I give away pies for every occasion," says Loretta, "they are my trademark."

CRUST
> 9-inch Classic Crisco® Double
> Crust

FILLING

4½ cups fresh blueberries, divided
  ½ cup granulated sugar
  ½ cup firmly packed brown sugar
  2 tablespoons plus 1½ teaspoons
    cornstarch
  ½ teaspoon cinnamon
  ⅛ teaspoon salt

1 tablespoon butter or margarine
1 teaspoon peach schnapps
2 tablespoons quick-cooking
  tapioca
4 to 5 drops red food color
  (optional)

DECORATIONS (optional)
> Reserved dough

2 tablespoons melted vanilla
  frozen yogurt

1. **For crust,** prepare (see pages 52–53). Roll and press bottom crust into 9-inch pie plate. Do not bake. Reserve dough scraps for decorations, if desired. Heat oven to 425°F.

2. **For filling,** place ½ cup blueberries in resealable plastic sandwich bag. Crush berries. Pour juice and berries into strainer over liquid measuring cup. Press berries to extract all juice. Pour water over berries until juice measures ½ cup.

3. Combine granulated sugar, brown sugar, cornstarch, cinnamon and salt in large saucepan. Add blueberry juice mixture. Cook and stir on medium heat until mixture comes to a boil. Remove from heat. Stir in butter and schnapps. Set pan in cold water about 5 minutes to cool. Stir in tapioca. Add food color, if desired. Stir in remaining blueberries carefully. Spoon into unbaked pie crust. Moisten pastry edge with water.

4. Roll top crust same as bottom. Lift onto filled pie. Trim ½ inch beyond edge of pie plate. Fold top edge under bottom crust. Flute.

5. **For decorations,** cut stars and diamonds from reserved dough. Dip cutouts in melted yogurt. Place on top of pie and around edge. Cut slits in top crust to allow steam to escape.

6. Bake at 425°F for 15 minutes. Cover cutouts and edge of pie with foil, if necessary, to prevent overbrowning. *Reduce oven temperature to 375°F.* Bake 20 to 25 minutes or until filling in center is bubbly and crust is golden brown. Cool to room temperature before serving.
      One 9-inch Pie

★ PEACH DELIGHT PIE ★

Michelle Neumiller, Casper, Wyoming
*Championship cooking must run in this family's blood because
Michelle is the daughter of last year's Wyoming winner, Joan
Neumiller.*

FILLING

2½ cups sliced, peeled peaches
    (about 1¼ pounds or
    2 to 3 large)
¾ cup granulated sugar

¼ cup quick-cooking tapioca
1 teaspoon lemon juice
1 teaspoon peach-flavored brandy

CRUMB MIXTURE

¼ cup all-purpose flour
¼ cup firmly packed brown sugar
¼ cup chopped almonds

3 tablespoons butter or
    margarine, melted

CRUST

9-inch Classic Crisco® Double
Crust

GLAZE

1 egg white, lightly beaten

Granulated sugar

1. **For filling,** combine peaches, granulated sugar, tapioca, lemon juice and brandy in medium bowl. Stir well. Let stand while making crumb mixture and crust.

2. **For crumb mixture,** combine flour, brown sugar, nuts and butter. Mix until crumbly.

3. Heat oven to 425°F.

4. **For crust,** prepare (see pages 52–53). Roll and press bottom crust into 9-inch pie plate. Do not bake. Sprinkle half of crumb mixture over unbaked pie crust. Add filling. Top with remaining crumbs.

5. Roll top crust same as bottom. Cut out heart shapes with cookie cutter. Place on filling around edge of pie.

6. **For glaze,** brush cutouts with egg white. Sprinkle with granulated sugar. Cover edge of pie with foil to prevent overbrowning.

7. Bake at 425°F for 10 minutes. *Reduce oven temperature to 350°F.* Bake 25 minutes. Remove foil. Bake 5 minutes. Serve barely warm or at room temperature.
              One 9-inch Pie

★ CHIP OFF THE OLD PIE ★

Mark Beridon, Baton Rouge, Louisiana
This Louisiana native has been cooking since he was 5 years old.

CRUST
    9-inch Classic Crisco® Single
    Crust

FILLING
    2 cups mashed, cooked sweet
        potatoes or yams
    ¼ cup sugar
    1 teaspoon cinnamon
    ½ teaspoon ginger
    ½ teaspoon nutmeg
    ½ teaspoon salt
    1 can (14 ounces) sweetened
        condensed milk
    2 eggs

TOPPING
    2 large raw sweet potatoes or
        yams
    2¼ cups Crisco® Shortening
    2 teaspoons cinnamon-sugar
        blend*
    ⅓ cup honey
    ½ cup toasted chopped pecans**

1. **For crust,** prepare (see pages 52–53). Do not bake. Heat oven to 350°F.

2. **For filling,** combine mashed sweet potatoes, sugar, cinnamon, ginger, nutmeg and salt in large bowl. Beat at medium speed of electric mixer until smooth. Combine sweetened condensed milk and eggs in separate bowl. Add to potato mixture. Beat until blended. Spoon into unbaked pie crust.

3. Bake at 350°F for 45 minutes or until knife inserted in center comes out clean. Cool to room temperature.

4. **For topping,** peel and very thinly slice sweet potatoes. Place in cold water 30 minutes or longer. Heat Crisco in large heavy saucepan to 365°F to 375°F. Dry potato slices. Fry a few at a time about 3 to 4 minutes or until crisp. Remove with slotted spoon. Drain on paper towels. Mound sweet potato chips on top of pie. Sprinkle with cinnamon-sugar blend. Drizzle with honey. Sprinkle with nuts. Refrigerate leftover pie.   *One 9-inch Pie*

*Use packaged cinnamon-sugar blend available in spice section or combine 1½ teaspoons sugar with ½ teaspoon cinnamon.

**To toast pecans, place in baking pan in 350°F oven for 5 to 7 minutes, stirring occasionally until toasted. Cool before using.

Note: For ease in cutting, remove topping along cutting lines.

★ CARAMEL APPLE CRUMB PIE ★

Chris Rienecker, Indianapolis, Indiana
Baking is therapeutic for Chris. "Baking cheers me up," she says, "it really makes me happy."

CRUST
9-inch Classic Crisco® Single Crust

2 tablespoons fine, dry bread crumbs

FILLING
9 cups sliced, peeled (½-inch slices) Granny Smith apples (about 3 pounds or 6 large)
½ teaspoon cinnamon
2 tablespoons water
3 tablespoons all-purpose flour
1 cup plus 3 tablespoons firmly packed brown sugar

½ cup whipping cream
2 tablespoons butter or margarine
1 teaspoon vanilla
¼ teaspoon almond extract

TOPPING
½ cup all-purpose flour
½ cup granulated sugar
½ cup fine, dry bread crumbs

½ teaspoon cinnamon
5 tablespoons butter or margarine, chilled

GLAZE
¼ cup reserved brown sugar syrup

¼ cup confectioners sugar

1. **For crust,** prepare (see pages 52–53). Sprinkle pie crust with 2 tablespoons bread crumbs. Do not bake. Heat oven to 425°F.

2. **For filling,** place apples in large skillet. Sprinkle with cinnamon and water. Cover. Steam on medium heat 7 minutes or until tender, stirring 2 or 3 times. Spoon apples and any liquid into large bowl. Sprinkle with 3 tablespoons flour. Toss gently.

3. Combine brown sugar, whipping cream and 2 tablespoons butter in small saucepan. Cook and stir on medium heat until mixture comes to a boil. Boil 3 minutes. Remove from heat. Stir in vanilla and almond extract. Reserve ¼ cup brown sugar syrup for glaze. Add remaining syrup to apples. Toss. Cool.

4. **For topping,** combine ½ cup flour, granulated sugar, ½ cup bread crumbs and ½ teaspoon cinnamon in medium bowl. Cut in 5 tablespoons butter until crumbly.

5. Spoon apple mixture into unbaked pie crust. Sprinkle with topping.

6. Bake at 425°F for 15 minutes. *Reduce oven temperature to 375°F.* Bake 40 minutes or until filling in center is bubbly and crust is golden brown. Cover edge with foil, if necessary, to prevent overbrowning. Cool slightly.

7. **For glaze,** reheat reserved ¼ cup brown sugar syrup. Add confectioners sugar. Beat well. Drizzle over pie. Serve warm. Refrigerate leftover pie.

One 9-inch Pie

★ OHIO SOUR CHERRY PIE ★

Diane Cordial, Powell, Ohio
Diane's pie was the national winner at the 1991 Crisco American
Pie Celebration.

FILLING
1¼ cups sugar
¼ cup cornstarch
1 bag (20 ounces) frozen dry
    pack pitted red tart cherries
    (4 cups)

2 tablespoons butter or
    margarine
¾ teaspoon vanilla
½ teaspoon almond extract
1 or 2 drops red food color
    (optional)

CRUST
3 cups all-purpose flour
1 tablespoon plus 1½ teaspoons
    sugar
1 teaspoon salt
1 cup plus 2 tablespoons Crisco®
    Shortening

½ cup water
1 egg, lightly beaten
1 tablespoon vinegar

GLAZE
1 tablespoon milk

½ teaspoon sugar

1. **For filling,** combine 1¼ cups sugar and cornstarch in medium saucepan. Stir in cherries gently. Cook and stir on medium or medium-high heat about 10 minutes or until mixture comes to a boil and is thickened and clear. Remove from heat. Stir in butter, vanilla, almond extract and red food color, if desired. Cool 1 hour.

2. **For crust,** combine flour, 1 tablespoon plus 1½ teaspoons sugar and salt in large bowl. Cut in Crisco using pastry blender (or 2 knives) until all flour is blended to form pea-size chunks.

3. Combine water, egg and vinegar in small bowl. Sprinkle over flour mixture, 1 tablespoon at a time. Toss lightly with fork until dough will form a ball. (You may not use all of liquid.) Divide dough into thirds. Form three 5- to 6-inch "pancakes." Wrap 1 in plastic wrap. Refrigerate or freeze for later use.

4. Heat oven to 375°F.

5. Roll and press bottom crust into 9-inch pie plate (see pages 52–53). Spoon filling into unbaked pie crust. Moisten pastry edge with water.

6. Roll top crust same as bottom. Cut the word OHIO or other design in center of crust. Lift crust onto filled pie. Trim ½ inch beyond edge of pie plate. Fold top edge under bottom crust. Flute. Add leaf cutouts.

7. **For glaze,** brush with milk. Sprinkle with ½ teaspoon sugar.

8. Bake at 375°F for 35 to 40 minutes or until filling in center is bubbly and crust is golden brown. Serve warm or at room temperature.   *One 9-inch Pie*

★ PEANUT SUPREME PIE ★

Violet La Breque, Leesburg, Virginia
This is the second consecutive win for Violet in Crisco's American
Pie Celebration.

CRUST
9-inch Classic Crisco® Single
Crust

PEANUT LAYER
½ cup chopped peanuts
½ cup Jif® Creamy Peanut Butter

½ cup confectioners sugar
½ cup half-and-half

FILLING
1 can (14 ounces) sweetened
condensed milk
½ cup Jif® Creamy Peanut Butter
1 cup milk

1 package (6-serving size) vanilla
flavor instant pudding and
pie filling mix (not sugar-free)

TOPPING
¾ cup chopped peanuts

1. **For crust,** prepare (see pages 52–53). Do not bake. Heat oven to 400°F.

2. **For peanut layer,** combine ½ cup nuts, peanut butter, confectioners sugar
and half-and-half in medium bowl. Stir until well blended. Pour into unbaked
pie crust.

3. Bake at 400°F for 20 to 25 minutes or until crust is golden brown. Cool
completely.

4. **For filling,** combine sweetened condensed milk and peanut butter in large
bowl. Beat at low speed of electric mixer until well blended. Add milk slowly.
Add pudding mix. Increase speed to medium. Beat 2 minutes. Pour over cooled
peanut layer.

5. **For topping,** sprinkle ¾ cup nuts over filling. Refrigerate 1 hour or more.

One 9-inch Pie

★ MINNESOTA'S FRESH BLUEBERRY ★ CREAM CHEESE PIE

Marjorie Johnson, Robbinsdale, Minnesota
"I just live in my kitchen," says Marjorie, "I have places for everything." Now she'll need to find a place for her blue ribbon.

CRUST
9-inch Classic Crisco® Double Crust

Milk or cream
Sugar

FILLING
¾ cup plus 2 tablespoons sugar
2 tablespoons cornstarch
⅛ teaspoon salt
1 tablespoon lemon juice

3 cups fresh blueberries, divided
2 tablespoons butter or margarine

CHEESE LAYER
1 package (3 ounces) cream cheese, softened
2 tablespoons sugar

¼ cup dairy sour cream
½ teaspoon grated lemon peel

DECORATIONS
Baked flower cutouts

7 blueberries

1. Heat oven to 425°F.

2. **For crust,** prepare (see pages 52–53). Press two thirds of dough between hands to form 5- to 6-inch "pancake." Form remaining dough into smaller "pancake." Roll and press larger "pancake" into 9-inch pie plate. Bake and cool completely.

3. Roll remaining dough to ⅛-inch thickness. Cut out seven 2-inch flowers using a cookie cutter. Cut ¼-inch hole in center of each. Place on ungreased baking sheet. Brush with milk. Sprinkle with sugar.

4. Bake at 425°F for 7 to 9 minutes or until lightly browned. Cool completely.

5. **For filling,** combine ¾ cup plus 2 tablespoons sugar, cornstarch and salt in medium saucepan. Add lemon juice and 1½ cups blueberries. Cook and stir on medium heat, until mixture comes to a boil. Simmer, stirring often, until thickened. Remove from heat. Stir in butter. Cool to room temperature. Fold in remaining 1½ cups blueberries.

6. **For cheese layer,** combine cream cheese, 2 tablespoons sugar, sour cream and lemon peel in small bowl. Beat at medium speed of electric mixer until smooth. Spread on bottom of baked pie crust. Spoon filling over cheese layer.

7. **For decorations,** place one flower cutout in center of pie and remaining 6 cutouts around edge of filling. Place 1 blueberry in center of each flower. Refrigerate.

One 9-inch Pie

★ HIGH COUNTRY PEACH PIE ★

Louise Kopasz, Pueblo, Colorado
Louise has won Crisco's American Pie Celebration competition at
the Colorado State Fair for a second consecutive year.

CRUST
9-inch Classic Crisco® Double
Crust

1 egg white, lightly beaten

FILLING
1 cup sugar
⅓ cup unbleached all-purpose
flour
3 tablespoons vanilla or French
vanilla flavor instant pudding
and pie filling mix (not
sugar-free)

2 tablespoons honey
5 cups sliced, peeled peaches
2 tablespoons Butter Flavor
Crisco®, divided

GLAZE
Milk

1. **For crust,** prepare (see pages 52–53). Roll and press bottom crust into
9-inch pie plate. Brush with egg white. Do not bake. Heat oven to 425°F.

2. **For filling,** combine sugar, flour, pudding mix and honey in large bowl.
Fold in peaches.

3. Melt 1 tablespoon Butter Flavor Crisco. Pour over peaches.

4. Lift peaches from liquid with slotted spoon, reserving ¼ cup liquid. Place
peaches and reserved liquid in unbaked pie crust. Dot with remaining 1
tablespoon Butter Flavor Crisco. Discard remaining liquid. Moisten pastry
edge with water.

5. Roll top crust same as bottom. Cut 5 peach leaf designs in center of pastry.
Reserve cutouts. Lift top crust onto filled pie. Trim ½ inch beyond edge of pie
plate. Fold top edge under bottom crust. Flute.

6. **For glaze,** brush with milk. Cut veins in leaf cutouts. Place between "leaf"
vents. Brush leaves with milk. Cover edge of crust with foil to prevent
overbrowning.

7. Bake at 425°F for 10 minutes. *Reduce oven temperature to 400°F. Bake 30*
minutes. Remove foil. Bake 5 minutes or until filling in center is bubbly and
crust is golden brown. Serve barely warm. *One 9-inch Pie*

★ ARIZONA'S SUPREME CITRUS PIE ★

Beth Sternitzky, Apache Junction, Arizona
This is the second consecutive year Beth has represented her state in
Crisco's American Pie Celebration.

CRUST
9-inch Classic Crisco® Single
Crust

FLUFFY FILLING
1 package (8 ounces) cream
    cheese, softened
1 can (14 ounces) sweetened
    condensed milk
1 can (6 ounces) frozen lemonade
    concentrate, thawed

1 package (4-serving size) lemon
    flavor instant pudding and
    pie filling mix (not sugar-free)
1 cup whipping cream, whipped

CLEAR FILLING
½ cup cornstarch
⅓ cup water
4 egg yolks
½ cup fresh lemon juice

1½ cups granulated sugar
1½ cups water
1 tablespoon butter or margarine

TOPPING
1 cup whipping cream
2 tablespoons confectioners sugar

¾ teaspoon vanilla

1. **For crust,** prepare and bake in 9- or 9½-inch deep-dish pie plate (see pages 52–53). Cool completely.

2. **For fluffy filling,** combine cream cheese and sweetened condensed milk in large bowl. Beat at low speed of electric mixer until smooth. Add lemonade concentrate. Blend well. Beat in pudding mix until smooth. Fold in whipped cream. Spoon into baked pie crust. Make shallow depression in filling 1 inch in from edge. Refrigerate.

3. **For clear filling,** combine cornstarch and ⅓ cup water in small bowl to form smooth paste. Combine egg yolks and lemon juice in medium bowl. Beat until smooth. Combine granulated sugar and 1½ cups water in medium saucepan. Cook on medium heat until mixture comes to a boil. Stir in cornstarch mixture slowly. Cook and stir until thickened and clear. Remove from heat. Stir in egg yolk mixture slowly until blended. Return to heat. Cook and stir 1 to 2 minutes or until mixture comes to a boil. Remove from heat. Stir in butter until blended. Cool completely. Spread gently over fluffy filling.

4. **For topping,** beat whipping cream in small bowl at high speed of electric mixer until stiff peaks form. Beat in confectioners sugar and vanilla. Spread over clear filling. Refrigerate until firm. *One 9- to 9½-inch Deep-Dish Pie*

★ APPLE BUTTERNUT PIE ★

Elizabeth Lincoln, West Rutland, Vermont
Elizabeth keeps her baking skills sharp by baking a pie every week.

CRUST
9-inch Crisco® Double Crust

FILLING
3½ cups chopped, peeled (½-inch pieces) Paula Red apples (about 1¼ pounds or 2 to 3 large)*
2 teaspoons lemon juice
1 cup light corn syrup
½ cup sugar

2 tablespoons butter or margarine, melted
3 eggs
¼ teaspoon salt
¼ cup chopped pitted dates
1 cup chopped butternuts**
⅛ teaspoon cinnamon
⅛ teaspoon nutmeg

DECORATIONS
¼ cup water
3 tablespoons sugar

Butternut halves

1. **For crust,** prepare (see pages 52–53). Roll and press bottom crust into 9-inch pie plate. Do not bake. Heat oven to 400°F.

2. **For filling,** toss apples and lemon juice in medium bowl.

3. Combine corn syrup, ½ cup sugar, butter, eggs and salt in small bowl. Beat at low speed of electric mixer until blended. Pour about ¾ cup in bottom of unbaked pie crust. Sprinkle dates over syrup layer. Sprinkle nuts over dates. Spoon apples over nuts. Drizzle remaining syrup over apples. Sprinkle cinnamon and nutmeg over top. Moisten pastry edge with water.

4. Roll top crust same as bottom. Lift onto filled pie. Trim ½ inch beyond edge of pie plate. Fold top edge under bottom crust. Flute. Form outline of an apple in center, using knife or tines of fork, and cut several small slits to allow steam to escape.

5. Bake at 400°F for 45 to 55 minutes or until filling in center is bubbly and crust is golden brown. Cover edge with foil, if necessary, to prevent overbrowning. Cool slightly.

6. **For decorations,** boil water and 3 tablespoons sugar in small saucepan until sugar dissolves and mixture is syrupy. Dip nuts in hot syrup. Arrange to frame apple outline on warm pie. (Tweezers may be helpful in glazing and arranging nuts.) Cool to room temperature before serving. Refrigerate leftover pie.

One 9-inch Pie

* Use Rome Beauty apples if Paula Red apples are not available.

** Use walnuts if butternuts are not available.

Party~Time Pies

★ LUSCIOUS CRANBERRY AND ★ BLUEBERRY PIE

Michele Delanty, Sunrise Beach, Missouri
In addition to baking daily for family and friends, Michele supplies
her husband's volunteer fire department meetings with cookies.

CRUST
9-inch Classic Crisco® Double Crust

½ teaspoon mace

FILLING
1 can (16 ounces) whole berry cranberry sauce
⅓ cup firmly packed brown sugar
¼ cup granulated sugar
2 tablespoons all-purpose flour
2 tablespoons cornstarch
2 tablespoons Citrus Hill® Orange Juice

½ teaspoon dried grated orange peel
⅛ teaspoon salt
2 cups fresh or frozen blueberries
2 tablespoons butter or margarine
1 egg, beaten

1. **For crust,** prepare (see pages 52–53) adding mace to flour mixture. Roll and press bottom crust into 9-inch pie plate. Do not bake. Reserve dough scraps for decorations, if desired. Heat oven to 425°F.

2. **For filling,** combine cranberry sauce, brown sugar, granulated sugar, flour, cornstarch, orange juice, orange peel and salt in large bowl. Stir in blueberries. Spoon into unbaked pie crust. Dot with butter. Moisten pastry edge with water.

3. Roll top crust same as bottom. Lift onto filled pie. Trim ½ inch beyond edge of pie plate. Fold top edge under bottom crust. Flute. Cut dogwood blossoms in top crust to allow steam to escape.

4. Cut flower or other shapes from reserved dough. Place on top of pie. Brush crust with egg.

5. Bake at 425°F for 40 minutes or until filling in center is bubbly and crust is golden brown. Cover edge with foil during last 10 minutes to prevent overbrowning. Cool to room temperature before serving.   *One 9-inch Pie*

Luscious Cranberry and Blueberry Pie

★ DATE-NUT PUMPKIN PIE ★

Ann Marshall, Hudson, Massachusetts
Although Ann claims that "apples are my specialty," pumpkin
worked for her this year with this extra special pumpkin pie.

CRUST
9-inch Classic Crisco® Single
Crust

DATE-NUT LAYER
1 package (8 ounces) pitted
    whole dates, chopped
¾ cup water
⅓ cup firmly packed brown sugar

¼ cup butter or margarine
½ cup chopped walnuts
½ teaspoon cinnamon

FILLING
2 eggs
1½ cups mashed, cooked or canned
    solid-pack pumpkin (not
    pumpkin pie filling)
½ cup granulated sugar
½ cup firmly packed brown sugar

1 cup evaporated milk
½ teaspoon cinnamon
½ teaspoon ginger
½ teaspoon nutmeg
¼ teaspoon salt
⅛ teaspoon cloves

GARNISH
Sweetened whipped cream

1. **For crust,** prepare (see pages 52–53). Do not bake. Reserve dough scraps for cutouts, if desired.* Heat oven to 450°F.

2. **For date-nut layer,** combine dates and water in medium saucepan. Cook on medium heat until mixture comes to a boil and dates have softened. Add ⅓ cup brown sugar and butter. Stir to blend. Remove from heat. Stir in nuts and cinnamon. Cool while preparing filling.

3. **For filling,** beat eggs lightly in medium bowl. Add pumpkin, granulated sugar, ½ cup brown sugar, evaporated milk, cinnamon, ginger, nutmeg, salt and cloves. Stir to blend.

4. Spoon date-nut mixture into unbaked pie crust. Pour in filling.

5. Bake at 450°F for 10 minutes. *Reduce oven temperature to 350°F.* Bake 35 minutes or until knife inserted in center comes out clean. Cool to room temperature before serving.

6. **For garnish,** spoon whipped cream around outer edge of pie just before serving. Refrigerate leftover pie. *One 9-inch Pie*

*Flute edge or cut small leaves and pumpkins from pastry scraps and press around edge of unbaked pie crust.

★ CITRUS DREAM PIE ★

Gloria Norton, Jacksonville, Florida
*Gloria is a 2-time winner of Crisco's American Pie Celebration in
Florida.*

CRUST
    9-inch Classic Crisco® Single
    Crust

3 to 4 tablespoons sesame seed,
    toasted

LEMON-ORANGE BUTTER FILLING
1½ cups sugar
    ¼ cup all-purpose flour
    ¼ cup cornstarch
    ⅛ teaspoon salt
    1 cup Citrus Hill® Orange Juice
    ¼ cup water

3 egg yolks, lightly beaten
2 tablespoons butter or
    margarine
1 teaspoon grated lemon peel
1 teaspoon grated orange peel
⅓ cup fresh lemon juice

LIME CREAM FILLING
    1 envelope (about 1 tablespoon)
        unflavored gelatin
    ¾ cup cold water, divided
    3 egg yolks
    ¾ cup sugar

2 packages (8 ounces each) cream
    cheese, softened
2 teaspoons grated lime peel
¼ cup fresh lime juice

TOPPING AND GARNISH
    1 cup whipping cream, whipped
    ½ cup reserved lemon-orange
        butter filling (optional)

1. **For crust,** prepare (see pages 52–53) adding sesame seed to flour mixture.
Bake and cool completely.

2. **For lemon-orange butter filling,** combine 1½ cups sugar, flour, cornstarch
and salt in medium saucepan. Stir orange juice and ¼ cup water into sugar
mixture gradually. Cook and stir on medium heat until mixture comes to a boil.
Reduce heat to low. Cook and stir 8 minutes. Stir ½ cup hot filling into egg
yolks slowly. Mix well. Return mixture to saucepan. Cook and stir on medium
heat until mixture comes to a boil. Reduce heat to low. Cook and stir 4
minutes. Remove from heat. Add butter. Stir well. Add lemon peel, orange peel
and lemon juice. Stir until blended. Cool.

3. **For lime cream filling,** sprinkle gelatin over ¼ cup water in small bowl. Beat
egg yolks lightly in small saucepan. Stir in ¾ cup sugar gradually. Add
remaining ½ cup water gradually. Stir well. Cook and stir on medium heat 5
minutes. Remove from heat. Add gelatin mixture, stirring until dissolved. Cool
2 to 3 minutes.

4. Beat cream cheese at medium speed of electric mixer until light and fluffy.
Add slightly cooled gelatin mixture gradually. Beat at low speed until blended.
Stir in lime peel and lime juice. Place in freezer 1 hour to set filling.

continued

Citrus Dream Pie

5. **To assemble pie,** spread half of lemon-orange butter filling in bottom of baked pie crust. Spoon lime cream filling over lemon-orange butter filling. Place in freezer 1 hour. Drop teaspoonfuls of remaining lemon-orange butter filling over lime filling, reserving ½ cup for garnish, if desired. Spread gently to cover.

6. **For garnish,** spread whipped cream carefully over top. Use reserved lemon-orange butter filling to pipe lattice strips across top, if desired. Refrigerate several hours or until firm.

One 9-inch Pie

★ SHOO-FLY PIE ★

Patricia S. Ziegler, Allentown, Pennsylvania
Long ago, Pennsylvania farmers developed the Shoo-Fly Pie, so
named because it was so sweet one had to "shoo away" the flies.

CRUST
    2 nine-inch Classic Crisco® Single
      Crusts

FILLING
    2 cups all-purpose flour
    1 cup sugar
    ½ cup Crisco® Shortening
    ⅔ cup dark corn syrup

    ⅓ cup light or dark molasses
    1 egg
    1 teaspoon baking soda
    1 cup warm water

1. **For crusts,** prepare (see pages 52–53). Do not bake. Heat oven to 400°F.

2. **For filling,** combine flour and sugar in large bowl. Cut in Crisco using pastry blender (or 2 knives) until mixture is crumbly.

3. Combine corn syrup, molasses and egg in medium bowl. Beat at low speed of electric mixer until blended.

4. Stir baking soda into water. Stir into molasses mixture. Stir in half of crumb mixture. Divide molasses mixture equally into 2 unbaked pie crusts. Sprinkle each with half of remaining crumbs.

5. Bake at 400°F for 10 minutes. *Reduce oven temperature to 350°F.* Bake 25 to 30 minutes or until set.

6. Serve warm or at room temperature. Refrigerate leftover pie.

Two 9-inch Pies

★ NEW HAMPSHIRE WHITE ★ MOUNTAIN PUMPKIN PIE

Nancy Labrie, Rye, New Hampshire
A self-taught cook, Nancy finds cooking to be a creative outlet.

CRUST
    9-inch Classic Crisco® Single
    Crust

NUT FILLING
    ⅔ cup chopped walnuts
    ⅓ cup firmly packed brown sugar
    ⅓ cup maple syrup

3 tablespoons butter or
    margarine

PUMPKIN FILLING
2½ cups mashed, cooked or canned
    solid-pack pumpkin (not
    pumpkin pie filling)
    1 cup evaporated milk
    3 egg yolks
    1 cup granulated sugar

2 tablespoons butter or
    margarine, melted
1 teaspoon cinnamon
1 teaspoon pumpkin pie spice
1 teaspoon vanilla
¼ teaspoon salt

MERINGUE
    3 egg whites
    ¼ teaspoon cream of tartar
    ¼ cup granulated sugar

2 tablespoons maple syrup, at
    room temperature

1. **For crust,** prepare (see pages 52–53). Do not bake. Heat oven to 425°F.

2. **For nut filling,** combine nuts, brown sugar, ⅓ cup maple syrup and 3 tablespoons butter in small saucepan. Cook and stir on medium heat until sugar is dissolved and nuts are glazed.

3. **For garnish,** if desired dip 3 or 4 walnut halves in filling to glaze. Spread thin coating of glaze on pastry leaf cutouts. Place on sheet of foil. Bake at 425°F until lightly browned. Cool. Pour nut filling into unbaked pie crust.

4. **For pumpkin filling,** combine pumpkin, evaporated milk, egg yolks, 1 cup granulated sugar, 2 tablespoons butter, cinnamon, pumpkin pie spice, vanilla and salt in large bowl. Beat at medium speed of electric mixer until blended. Pour over nut filling.

5. Bake at 425°F for 10 minutes. *Reduce oven temperature to 350°F.* Bake 50 minutes or until knife inserted in center comes out clean.

6. **For meringue,** beat egg whites and cream of tartar in medium bowl at high speed until foamy. Beat in ¼ cup granulated sugar and 2 tablespoons maple syrup, 1 tablespoon at a time. Beat until sugar is dissolved and stiff peaks form. Spread over filling, covering completely and sealing to edge of pie.

7. Bake at 350°F for 12 to 15 minutes or until golden. Cool to room temperature before serving. Refrigerate leftover pie.

One 9-inch Pie

★ CHERRY CITY AMARETTO ★ CHERRY CREAM PIE

Florence Neavoll, Salem, Oregon
This outstanding pie gets its name from Salem's nickname, The Cherry City.

CRUST
10-inch Classic Crisco® Single
Crust

CREAM LAYER

²/₃ cup granulated sugar
¼ cup cornstarch
¼ teaspoon salt
2 cups half-and-half

1 cup milk
3 egg yolks, lightly beaten
1 tablespoon butter or margarine
½ teaspoon almond extract

FILLING

1 can (16 ounces) pitted red tart
   cherries in water
½ cup reserved cherry liquid
²/₃ cup granulated sugar
2 tablespoons cornstarch
2 tablespoons all-purpose flour
⅛ teaspoon salt

1 tablespoon amaretto
1 teaspoon red food color
   (optional)
½ teaspoon fresh lemon juice
½ teaspoon vinegar
1 tablespoon butter or margarine

TOPPING

1½ teaspoons unflavored gelatin
2 tablespoons plus 2 teaspoons
   water
1½ cups whipping cream
6 tablespoons confectioners sugar

1 teaspoon almond extract
1 bar (1¼ ounces) white
   chocolate with almonds,
   shaved
Slivered almonds

1. **For crust,** prepare and bake (see pages 52–53). Cool completely.

2. **For cream layer,** combine ²/₃ cup granulated sugar, ¼ cup cornstarch and salt in medium saucepan. Stir in half-and-half and milk. Cook and stir on medium heat until mixture comes to a boil. Boil 1 minute. Remove from heat. Stir half of mixture into beaten egg yolks. Mix well. Return mixture to saucepan. Blend well. Boil and stir 1 minute. Remove from heat. Stir in butter and almond extract. Cool to room temperature. Refrigerate.

3. **For filling,** drain cherries, reserving ½ cup liquid. Pat cherries with paper towels. Combine ²/₃ cup granulated sugar, 2 tablespoons cornstarch, flour and salt in medium saucepan. Mix until smooth. Cook and stir on medium heat until mixture is thickened and clear. Add cherries. Cook and stir on low heat 10 to 15 minutes. Remove from heat. Stir in amaretto, food color, lemon juice, vinegar and butter. Cool to room temperature. *continued*

4. **For topping,** combine gelatin and water in very small saucepan. Cook and stir on low heat until gelatin dissolves. Cool until warm, but still liquid.

5. Beat whipping cream in medium bowl at high speed of electric mixer until soft peaks form. Beat in gelatin slowly. Beat in confectioners sugar and almond extract.

6. **To assemble pie,** spread cream layer in cooled pie crust. Cover with cherry filling. Pipe topping over filling in decorative fashion. Sprinkle with shaved chocolate and slivered nuts. Refrigerate. *One 10-inch Pie*

★ CHOCOLATE CHIP PECAN PIE ★

Janice Kyle, Oklahoma City, Oklahoma
Janice was encouraged to enter her pie in Crisco's American Pie
Celebration by her prize-winning sister, Rosalie Seebeck. Rosalie
won the national contest in 1989.

CRUST
  9-inch Classic Crisco® Single
  Crust

FILLING
  4 eggs
  1 cup sugar
  1 cup light corn syrup
  3 tablespoons butter or
    margarine, melted
  1 teaspoon vanilla

  ¼ teaspoon salt
  2 cups pecan halves
  ½ cup Hershey's Semi-Sweet
    Chocolate Chips
  1 tablespoon plus 1½ teaspoons
    bourbon, optional

1. **For crust,** prepare (see pages 52–53). Do not bake. Heat oven to 375°F.

2. **For filling,** beat eggs in large bowl at low speed of electric mixer until blended. Stir in sugar, corn syrup, butter, vanilla and salt with spoon until blended. Stir in nuts, chocolate chips and bourbon. Pour into unbaked pie crust.

3. Bake at 375°F for 55 to 60 minutes or until set. Cover edge with foil, if necessary, to prevent overbrowning. Cool to room temperature before serving. Refrigerate leftover pie. *One 9-inch Pie*

Chocolate Chip Pecan Pie

★ PEANUT CREAM PIE ★

Robyn Hogan, Albuquerque, New Mexico
Robyn set out to develop "a really different kind of pie." The result
won her a chance to represent New Mexico in Crisco's American Pie
Celebration.

CRUST
9-inch Classic Crisco® Single
Crust

CRUMB LAYER
⅓ cup Jif® Extra Crunchy Peanut   ½ cup confectioners sugar
Butter

FUDGE SAUCE
1 square (1 ounce) Hershey's   ⅓ cup plus ½ teaspoon boiling
Unsweetened Baking   water
Chocolate   ½ cup granulated sugar
1½ teaspoons butter or margarine   1 tablespoon light corn syrup
                                        ½ teaspoon vanilla

FILLING
½ cup granulated sugar   ½ cup peanut butter chips
⅓ cup all-purpose flour   2 tablespoons butter or
2 cups milk   margarine
3 egg yolks, lightly beaten   1 teaspoon vanilla

TOPPING
1½ cups whipping cream   ½ teaspoon vanilla
1½ teaspoons granulated sugar

DRIZZLE
¼ cup peanut butter chips   ½ teaspoon Crisco® Shortening

1. **For crust,** prepare and bake (see pages 52–53). Cool completely.

2. **For crumb layer,** combine peanut butter and confectioners sugar in small
bowl. Stir with fork until crumbly.

3. **For fudge sauce,** combine chocolate and 1½ teaspoons butter in small
saucepan. Cook on low heat until chocolate melts. Stir in water. Add ½ cup
granulated sugar and corn syrup. Stir well. Increase heat to medium. Cook until
mixture simmers. Cover. Simmer 3 minutes. Do not stir. Uncover. Reduce heat
to medium-low. Simmer 2 minutes without stirring. Stir in ½ teaspoon vanilla.
Cool until slightly warm.

4. **For filling,** combine ½ cup granulated sugar and flour in medium saucepan.
Stir in milk. Cook and stir on medium-high heat until mixture comes to a boil.
Cook and stir 2 minutes. Remove from heat. Stir about one third of hot
mixture slowly into egg yolks. Mix well. Return mixture to saucepan. Cook and
stir 2 minutes. Remove from heat. Add ½ cup peanut butter chips, 2 tablespoons
butter and 1 teaspoon vanilla. Stir until chips are melted.   *continued*

Peanut Cream Pie

5. Sprinkle crumb layer into baked pie crust. Pour fudge sauce over crumbs. Spoon filling over fudge sauce. Cover with plastic wrap. Refrigerate until set, about 2 to 3 hours.

6. **For topping,** combine whipping cream, 1½ teaspoons granulated sugar and ½ teaspoon vanilla in medium bowl. Beat at high speed of electric mixer until stiff peaks form. Spread over filling. Refrigerate.

7. **For drizzle,** combine ¼ cup peanut butter chips and Crisco in small microwave-safe cup. Microwave at 50% (MEDIUM) 1 minute. Stir. Repeat until smooth (or melt on rangetop in small saucepan on very low heat). Drizzle over whipped cream. Cut into wedges immediately before drizzle hardens. Serve or store in refrigerator.   *One 9-inch Pie*

★ RHUBARB, APPLE AND ★ PINEAPPLE PIE

Louise E. Davis, Dallas, Texas
Louise has been entering contests for over 30 years and has won over
250 ribbons for her baking and knitting, her other hobby.

CRUST
    9-inch Classic Crisco® Double
    Crust

FILLING
    1 cup sugar
    3 tablespoons all-purpose flour
    ⅛ teaspoon salt
    1 cup chopped, peeled McIntosh
        apple (about ⅓ pound or
        1 medium)
    1 teaspoon lemon juice

    2 cups fresh or frozen cut
        rhubarb (½-inch pieces)
    ½ cup drained canned crushed
        pineapple
    ¼ cup honey
    1 tablespoon butter or margarine

1. **For crust,** prepare (see pages 52–53). Roll and press bottom crust into 9- to 9½-inch deep-dish pie plate, leaving overhang. Do not bake. Heat oven to 450°F.

2. **For filling,** combine sugar, flour and salt in small bowl. Place apple in large bowl. Sprinkle with lemon juice. Add rhubarb, pineapple and sugar mixture. Toss to coat. Spoon filling into unbaked pie crust. Drizzle with honey. Dot with butter. Moisten pastry edge with water. Cover pie with woven lattice top (see page 55).

3. Place pie in 450°F oven. *Reduce oven temperature to 350°F immediately.* Bake for 1 hour to 1 hour 15 minutes or until filling in center is bubbly and crust is golden brown. Cool to room temperature before serving.

                                            One 9- or 9½-inch Deep-Dish Pie

★ CHERRY PIE ★

Eunice Ruth, Rising City, Nebraska
Eunice is a veteran cooking and baking competitor. She has entered
as many as 34 different cooking and baking competitions in a
single year.

FILLING
1 bag (20 ounces) frozen dry
pack pitted red tart cherries
(4 cups)
1½ cups sugar, divided
⅓ cup cornstarch
⅛ teaspoon salt
½ cup reserved cherry juice

½ cup raspberry juice blend or
cocktail
1 tablespoon butter or margarine
½ teaspoon red food color
(optional)
¼ teaspoon almond extract

CRUST
9-inch Classic Crisco® Double
Crust

TOPPING
Sugar

1. **For filling,** thaw and thoroughly drain cherries, reserving juice.

2. **For crust,** prepare (see pages 52–53). Roll and press bottom crust into 9-inch pie plate. Do not bake. Heat oven to 375°F.

3. Combine ¾ cup sugar, cornstarch and salt in medium saucepan. Add ½ cup reserved cherry juice and raspberry juice. Cook and stir on medium heat until mixture is thickened and smooth. Remove from heat. Add remaining ¾ cup sugar, butter, food color, almond extract and cherries. Stir until sugar is dissolved. Spoon into unbaked pie crust. Moisten pastry edge with water.

4. Roll top crust same as bottom. Lift onto filled pie. Trim ½ inch beyond edge of pie plate. Fold top edge under bottom crust. Flute. Cut slits in top crust to allow steam to escape. Cover edge with foil to prevent overbrowning.

5. **For topping,** sprinkle lightly with sugar.

6. Bake at 375°F for 50 to 60 minutes or until filling in center is bubbly and crust is golden brown. Serve warm or at room temperature.   *One 9-inch Pie*

Note: A woven lattice top (see page 55) can be made for top crust, if desired.

★ CIDER APPLE PIE IN ★ CHEDDAR CRUST

Mary Lou Tuckwiller, Lewisburg, West Virginia
Mary Lou has taken the traditional taste of sweet and succulent
apple pie and contrasted it with the sharp taste of Cheddar cheese in
this terrific pie.

CRUST
2 cups sifted all-purpose flour
1 cup shredded Cheddar cheese
1/2 teaspoon salt

2/3 cup Crisco® Shortening
5 to 6 tablespoons ice water

FILLING
6 cups sliced, peeled apples (about 2 pounds or 6 medium)
1 cup apple cider
2/3 cup sugar

2 tablespoons cornstarch
2 tablespoons water
1/2 teaspoon cinnamon
1 tablespoon butter or margarine

GLAZE
1 egg yolk

1 tablespoon water

1. Heat oven to 400°F.

2. **For crust,** place flour, cheese and salt in food processor bowl. Add Crisco. Process 15 seconds. Sprinkle water through food chute, 1 tablespoon at a time, until dough just forms (process time not to exceed 20 seconds). Shape into ball. Divide dough in half. Press between hands to form two 5- to 6-inch "pancakes." Roll and press bottom crust into 9-inch pie plate.

3. **For filling,** combine apples, apple cider and sugar in large saucepan. Cook and stir on medium-high heat until mixture comes to a boil. Reduce heat to low. Simmer 5 minutes. Combine cornstarch, 2 tablespoons water and cinnamon. Stir into apples. Cook and stir until mixture comes to a boil. Remove from heat. Stir in butter. Spoon into unbaked pie crust. Moisten pastry edge with water.

4. Roll top crust same as bottom. Lift onto filled pie. Trim 1/2 inch beyond edge of pie plate. Fold top edge under bottom crust. Flute. Cut slits or design in top crust to allow steam to escape.

5. **For glaze,** beat egg yolk with fork. Stir in 1 tablespoon water. Brush over top.

6. Bake at 400°F for 35 to 40 minutes or until filling in center is bubbly and crust is golden brown. Cover edge with foil, if necessary, to prevent overbrowning Cool to room temperature before serving.   *One 9-inch Pie*

Note: Golden Delicious, Granny Smith and Jonathan apples are all suitable for pie baking.

Cider Apple Pie in Cheddar Crust

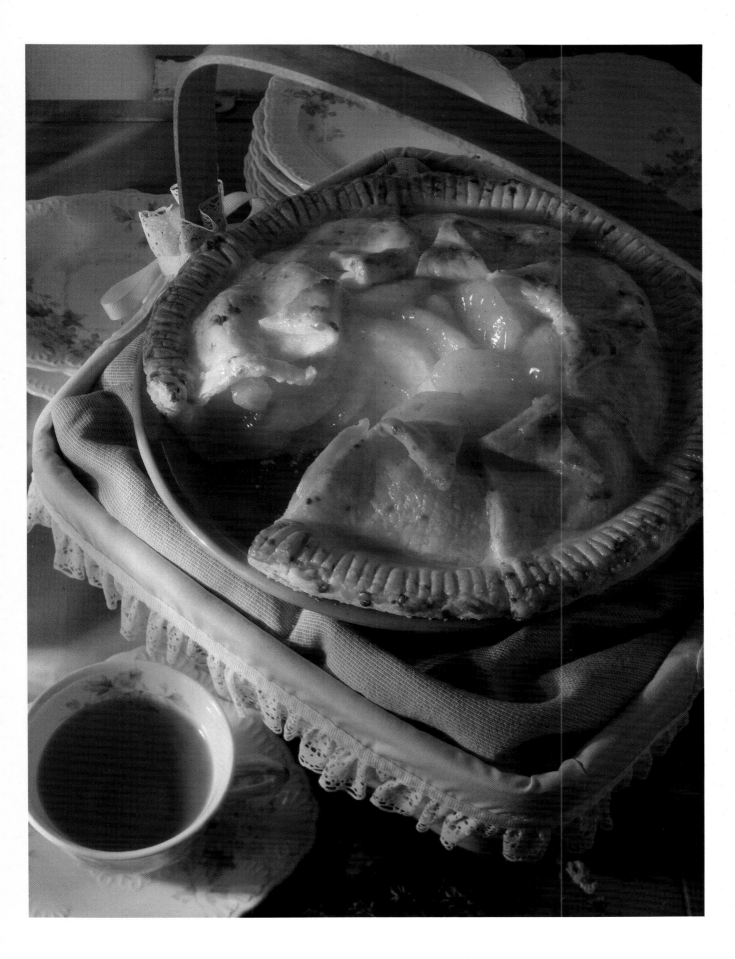

★ CRISCO'S DOOR COUNTY ★ CHERRY PIE

Susan M. Vlazny, New Berlin, Wisconsin
The secret to this combination cheesecake-cherry pie is a layer of
luscious cherries.

FILLING
2 cans (16 ounces each) pitted
   red tart cherries in water
1 cup sugar
¼ cup cornstarch
1 cup reserved cherry liquid

CRUST
9-inch Classic Crisco® Single
   Crust

CREAM CHEESE LAYER
1 package (8 ounces) cream
   cheese, softened
½ cup sugar
½ teaspoon vanilla
2 eggs

TOPPING
1½ cups dairy sour cream

1. **For filling,** drain cherries, reserving 1 cup liquid. Combine 1 cup sugar and cornstarch in medium saucepan. Stir in 3 cups cherries and 1 cup reserved liquid. Set aside remaining cherries and liquid for another use. Cook and stir on medium-high heat until mixture comes to a boil. Boil 1 minute. Cool while preparing crust.

2. **For crust,** prepare (see pages 52–53). Do not bake. Heat oven to 425°F.

3. Spoon half of cherry filling into unbaked pie crust.

4. Bake at 425°F for 15 minutes.

5. **For cream cheese layer,** beat cream cheese, ½ cup sugar and vanilla in small bowl at medium speed of electric mixer until smooth. Beat in eggs until blended.

6. Spoon cream cheese mixture over cherry filling.

7. *Reduce oven temperature to 350°F.* Return pie to oven. Bake 25 minutes. Cool to room temperature. Top with remaining cherry mixture.

8. **For topping,** place spoonfuls of sour cream around edge of pie. Refrigerate leftover pie.
One 9-inch Pie

Index